Graph-related Optimization and Decision Support Systems

FOCUS SERIES

Series Editor
Jean-Charles Pomerol

Graph-related Optimization and Decision Support Systems

Saoussen Krichen
Jouhaina Chaouachi

WILEY

First published 2014 in Great Britain and the United States by ISTE Ltd and John Wiley & Sons, Inc.

ISTE Ltd
27-37 St George's Road
London SW19 4EU
UK

www.iste.co.uk

John Wiley & Sons, Inc.
111 River Street
Hoboken, NJ 07030
USA

www.wiley.com

Library of Congress Control Number: 2014941565

British Library Cataloguing-in-Publication Data
A CIP record for this book is available from the British Library
ISSN 2051-2481 (Print)
ISSN 2051-249X (Online)
ISBN 978-1-84821-743-0

Contents

List of Tables

List of Figures

List of Algorithms

Introduction

Constrained optimization is a challenging branch of operations research that aims to create a model which has a wide range of applications in the supply chain, telecommunication and medical fields. The problem structure is split into two main components: the objective(s) to accomplish and the feasible set framed by the system constraints. The aim of this book is to expose optimization problems that can be expressed as a graph, by detailing, for each problem studied, the set of nodes and the set of edges. We propose an incentive to design a platform that integrates all optimization components in order to output the best solution regarding the parameters' tuning. We propose in our analysis, for optimization problem, to provide its graph modeling and mathematical formulation and expose some of its variants. As solution approaches, an optimizer can be the most promising way of limited sizes of the instances. For large problem instances, approximate algorithms are the most appropriate way of generating high-quality solutions. We propose, for each problem studied, a greedy algorithm as a problem-specific heuristic and a genetic algorithm as a metaheuristic.

One of the most simple-structured optimization problems is the knapsack problem. Known to be a master problem, it consists of a partial packing of a set of items in one or several knapsacks with fixed capacities. Despite its simple structure, the knapsack problem is $\mathcal{NP}$-hard. Therefore, alternative solution approaches are required, depending on the problem size of the addressed instance.

The bin packing problem is a combinatorial optimization problem that has attracted many researchers during the last three decades. The problem consists of packing a set of items into a minimum number of bins while respecting the capacity constraints of each bin. Apart from its theoretical interest, the bin packing problem performs well in modeling a large variety of real-world applications such as computer science, production planning and logistics. Since then, the problem has been broken down into several different versions based on various factors such as geometry of the objects, number of bins, dimensionality, nature of the problem and its constraints. We follow the same study outline for the bin packing and enumerate specifically designed heuristics as the first-fit and the next-fit algorithms. The genetic algorithm adapted to the bin packing is proved to be very effective in solving packing problems.

The assignment problem is also detailed in this book as an alternative way for formulating the total and partial packing. We show its modeling as a graph that well shows the assignment of agents to jobs.

The resource-constrained project scheduling problem is a well-known problem in scheduling theory and is an appropriate modeling of many applications such as manpower scheduling, grid computing, classroom arrangement and the surveillance problem. It is widely known to be notoriously difficult to solve due to the employment of scarce resources as well as precedence relations between activities. Considering these constraints, the problem consists of finding an efficient arrangement of activities that leads to a minimal completion time of the project. The greedy algorithm and the genetic algorithm are likewise developed for solving the resource-constrained project scheduling problem. The spanning tree problem consists of considering a connected valued graph and trying to generate the minimum-valued tree that encompasses all nodes of the graph. Numerous algorithms are provided to get such a tree as well as a genetic algorithm. A decision support system (DSS) is designed and developed to handle optimization problems as the knapsack and routing problems. We illustrate the need of a DSS by addressing a real routing application that incorporates numerous optimization algorithms in the north west of Tunisia.

1

Basic Concepts in Optimization and Graph Theory

1.1. Introduction

An optimization problem is a formal specification of a set of proposals related to a specific framework that includes one or numerous decision makers, one or several objectives to be achieved and a set of structural constraints. Optimization has been practiced in numerous fields of study as it provides a primary tool for modeling and solving complex and hard constrained problems. After the 1960s, integer programming formulations and approximate approaches have received considerable attention as useful tools for solving optimization problems. Depending on the problem structure and its complexity, appropriate solution approaches were proposed to generate appropriate solutions in a reasonable computation time. Several optimization studies are formulated as a problem whose goal is to find the best solution, which corresponds to the minimum or maximum value of a single-objective function. The challenge of solving combinatorial problems lies in their computational complexity since most of them are non-deterministic polynomial-time (NP)-hard [GAR 79]. This complexity can mainly be expressed in terms of the relationship between the search space and the difficulty of finding a solution. The search space in combinatorial optimization problems is discrete and multidimensional. The higher the dimensionality, the larger the search space, and the harder the problem. The remainder of this chapter is organized as follows. In section 1.2, we highlight the terminology adopted throughout this book. Section 1.3 deals with the mathematical structure of an optimization problem and enumerates its main variants. Section 1.4 illustrates the previously announced principles by a didactic example. Section 1.5 outlines the main features of an optimization problem.

1.2. Notation

We present in the following the major symbols used for defining an optimization problem:

Symbols	Description
n	the number of decision variables
k	the number of objectives
$x = (x_1, \ldots, x_n)^T$	the vector of decision variables
$c_{(p,n)}$	the cost matrix
A	the matrix of constraints
B	Resources limitations
E_O	The set of efficient solutions in the objective space
E_D	The set of efficient solutions in the decision space

1.3. Problem structure and variants

Assuming the linearity of an optimization problem, its mathematical modeling is outlined as follows:

$$Max \quad p.x \qquad\qquad [1.1]$$

$$S.t. \ A.x \le B \qquad\qquad [1.2]$$

$$x \in \mathcal{X} \qquad\qquad [1.3]$$

where $x = (x_1, \ldots, x_n)^T$ denotes the vector of decision variables, p, b and A are constant vectors and matrix of coefficients, respectively.

Many variants of this formulation can be pointed out:

– *Continuous linear programming (CLP)*: The optimization model [1.1]-[1.3] is a CLP if the decision variables are continuous. For continuous linear optimization problems, efficient exact algorithms such as the simplex-type method [BUR 12] or interior point methods exist [ANS 12].

– *Integer linear programming (ILP)*: The optimization model [1.1]-[1.3] is an ILP if $\mathcal{X}$ is the set of feasible integer solutions (i.e. decision variables are discrete). This class of models is very important as many real-life applications are modeled with discrete variables since their handled resources are indivisible (as cars, machines and containers). A large number of combinatorial optimization problems can be formulated as ILPs (e.g. packing problems, scheduling problems and traveling salesman) in which the decision variables are discrete and the search space is finite. However, the objective function and constraints may take any form [PAP 82].

– *Mixed integer programming (MIP)*: The optimization model [1.1]-[1.4] is called MIP, when the decision variables are both discrete and continuous. Consequently, MIP models generalize the CLP and ILP models. MIP problems have improved dramatically of late with the use of advanced optimization techniques such as relaxations and decomposition approaches, branch-and-bound, and cutting plane algorithms when the problem sizes are small [GAR 12, WAN 13, COO 11]. Metaheuristics are also a good candidate for larger instances. They can also be used to generate good lower or upper bounds for exact algorithms and improve their efficiency.

1.4. Features of an optimization problem

Optimization problems can be classified in terms of the nature of the objective function and the nature of the constraints. Special forms of the objective function and the constraints give rise to specialized models that can efficiently model the problem under study. From this point of view, various types of optimization models can be highlighted: linear and nonlinear, single and multiobjective optimization problems, and continuous and combinatorial programming models. Based on such features, we have to define the following points:

– *The number of decision makers*: if one decision maker (DM) is involved, the problem dealt with is an *optimization problem*; otherwise we are concerned with a *game* that can be cooperative or non-cooperative, depending on the DMs' standpoints.

– *The number of objectives*: it determines the nature of the solution to be generated. If only one objective is addressed in the decision problem, the best solution corresponds to the optimal solution. However, if more than one objective is considered, we went to generate a set of efficient solutions that correspond to some trade-offs between the objectives under study.

– *The linearity*: when both the objective(s) and the constraints are linear, the optimization problem is said to be linear. In that case, specific solution approaches can be adapted as the simplex method. Otherwise, the problem is nonlinear in which case the resolution becomes more complex and the decision space is not convex.

– *The nature of the decision variables*: if the decision variables are integer, we deal with a combinatorial optimization problem.

1.5. A didactic example

Let us consider the following optimization problem involving two decision variables x_1 and x_2. We show in this illustrative example how the solution changes in terms of the nature of the decision variables that can be either continuous or binary and the number of objectives $k = 1$, 2. Hence, four optimization problems follow:

	$k = 1$	$k = 2$
$x_1, x_2 \geq 0$	$\begin{aligned} Max \quad & 2x_1 + x_2 \\ S.t. \quad & 5x_1 + 7x_2 \leq 100 \\ & x_1 - 3x_2 \leq 80 \\ & x \geq 0 \end{aligned}$ $\Rightarrow$	
	$\boxed{\begin{aligned} (x_1, x_2) &= (20, 0) \\ z(x) &= 40 \end{aligned}}$	$\begin{aligned} Max \quad & 2x_1 + x_2 \\ & x_1 + 5x_2 \\ S.t. \quad & 5x_1 + 7x_2 \leq 100 \\ & x_1 - 3x_2 \leq 80 \\ & x \geq 0 \end{aligned}$ $\Downarrow$ $\boxed{\begin{aligned} E_D &= \{(20,0),(0,14.285)\} \\ E_O &= \{\begin{pmatrix} 40 \\ 20 \end{pmatrix}\begin{pmatrix} 14.285 \\ 71.428 \end{pmatrix}\} \end{aligned}}$
$x_1, x_2 \in \{0, 1\}$	$\begin{aligned} Max \quad & 2x_1 + x_2 \\ S.t. \quad & 5x_1 + 7x_2 \leq 100 \\ & x_1 - 3x_2 \leq 80 \\ & x \in \{0, 1\} \end{aligned}$ $\Rightarrow$	
	$\boxed{\begin{aligned} (x_1, x_2) &= (1, 1) \\ z(x) &= 3 \end{aligned}}$	$\begin{aligned} Max \quad & 2x_1 + x_2 \\ & x_1 + 5x_2 \\ S.t. \quad & 5x_1 + 7x_2 \leq 100 \\ & x_1 - 3x_2 \leq 80 \\ & x \in \{0, 1\} \end{aligned}$ $\Downarrow$ $\boxed{\begin{aligned} E_D &= \{(1,1)\} \\ E_O &= \{\begin{pmatrix} 3 \\ 6 \end{pmatrix}\} \end{aligned}}$

As previously mentioned, the resolution of the single-objective optimization problem yields to the finding of the optimal solution that varies depending on the nature of the decision variables. However, if a second objective is added, the resolution generates a set of Pareto-optimal solutions, as it is the case for $k = 2$.

1.6. Basic concepts in graph theory

A graph G is defined as a couple of sets $G = (V, E)$: a vertex set V and an edge set E.

– *The vertex set* states all involved entities that model the original problem.

– *The edge set* is an exhaustive enumeration of all possible connections between two vertices. If $e = \{x, y\}$ is an edge, we say "x is adjacent to y". A graph can also contain a loop whose endpoints are equal. Based on such features, we can point out numerous types connections in a graph:

- *Simple edge*: a connection between two vertices x and y such that $x \neq y$. It is modeled as a set of two nodes $\{x, y\}$.

- *Oriented edge*: an edge represented by a couple of vertices (x, y).

- *Multiple edges*: numerous edges having the same pair of vertices.

- *Loop*: an edge whose endpoints are equal.

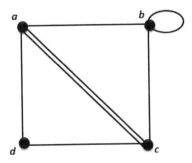

Figure 1.1. *An example of a graph with $n = 4$ and $e = 5$*

A simple graph is a graph that contains neither loops nor multiple edges. Simple graphs can be directed as shown in Figure 1.2(a), undirected as is the case of Figure 1.2(b) or/and weighted as shown in Figure 1.2(c). A weighted graph can designate a road network where each edge is labeled by the distance between the corresponding vertices. Weights can also express the traveling cost between two adjacent vertices.

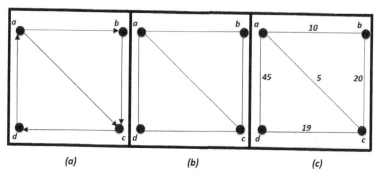

Figure 1.2. *Types of simple graphs*

1.6.1. *Degree of a graph*

The degree of a vertex x in a graph G, denoted by $d_{G(x)}$, is the number of edges where x is one of their endpoints. Note that $e = \frac{\sum_{x \in V} deg(x)}{2}$.

1.6.2. *Matrix representation of a graph*

An alternative representation of a graph is the matrix representation A that designates the adjacency matrix. It is a symmetric square matrix of order n if the graph is undirected. If the graph is weighted, the matrix reports the distances' values if the corresponding vertices are adjacent and 0 elsewhere. Table 1.1 corresponds to the matrix representations of graphs (a), (b) and (c) of Figure 1.2. The matrix representation is adopted mainly for handling a routing problem for which a shortest path has to be generated using the extracted adjacency matrix A.

Graph	(a)	(b)	(c)
Matrix	$\begin{pmatrix} 0\;1\;1\;0 \\ 0\;0\;1\;0 \\ 0\;0\;0\;1 \\ 1\;0\;0\;0 \end{pmatrix}$	$\begin{pmatrix} 0\;1\;1\;1 \\ 1\;0\;1\;0 \\ 1\;1\;0\;1 \\ 1\;0\;1\;0 \end{pmatrix}$	$\begin{pmatrix} 0\;\;10\;\;5\;\;45 \\ 10\;\;0\;\;20\;\;0 \\ 5\;\;20\;\;0\;\;19 \\ 45\;\;0\;\;19\;\;0 \end{pmatrix}$

Table 1.1. *Matrix representation of simple graphs*

1.6.3. *Connected graphs*

A graph G is said to be connected if there exists at least a path between each pair of vertices x and y:

$$\forall x, y \in V \exists \text{a path: } x \to \ldots \to y \qquad [1.4]$$

We can note that a basic result related to connected graphs is the following:

$$\text{If } e < n - 1, \text{ then } G \text{ is not connected} \qquad [1.5]$$

Based on equation [1.5], we can clearly understand that if $e \geq n-1$, G can be either connected or not. In fact, if we observe the graph of Figure 1.3, condition $\underbrace{e}_{8} \geq \underbrace{n-1}_{6}$ holds, but the graph is not connected. Whenever a graph is connected, we can speak about finding shortest paths between pairs of vertices. Routing problems address such topics that are mainly about minimizing the number of vehicles used and determining the shortest itinerary for each vehicle. An itinerary can be either a circuit as is the case of the basic vehicle routing problem or a path when we speak about the open vehicle routing problem.

1.6.4. *Itineraries in a graph*

When trying to choose the most cost-efficient solution, we should handle a weighted graph.

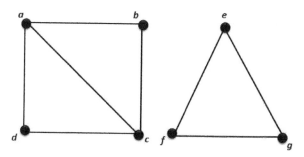

Figure 1.3. *A non-connected graph with* $n = 7$ *and* $e = 8$

A *path* is a succession of adjacent edges that starts from a predefined source x and ends at a destination y such that $x \neq y$. For an optimization problem, we generally speak about the least cost path.

A *circuit* is a path that starts and ends at the same vertex ($x = y$). The traveling salesman problem is the most famous optimization problem that tries to generate the least cost Hamiltonian circuit (a circuit that runs through all vertices of the graph) in the graph under study. Figure 2.1 reports a weighted connected graph with 7 vertices and 12 edges where the vertices correspond to the cities and the edges are direct routes weighted by their corresponding distances. The following are examples of itineraries:

Itinerary	Detail	Distance
Path	• $a \xrightarrow{10} b \xrightarrow{45} d \xrightarrow{12} e$	67
	• $a \xrightarrow{90} c \xrightarrow{24} e$	114
Circuit	• $a \xrightarrow{10} b \xrightarrow{45} e \xrightarrow{12} f \xrightarrow{24} c \xrightarrow{90} a$	181
	• $a \xrightarrow{90} c \xrightarrow{57} b \xrightarrow{10} a$	157

1.6.5. Tree graphs

A tree T is a connected graph that does not contain any circuit. The vertex set V contains:

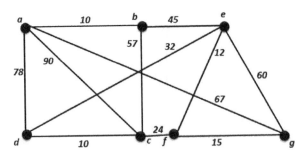

Figure 1.4. *A connex plutot connected graph with $n = 7$ and $e = 12$*

– intermediates nodes or branches: x is an intermediate node if $d_T(x) \geq 2$;

– leaves: x is a leave if $d_T(x) = 1$.

A graph $T = (V, E)$ is a tree if:

– there exists only one path between each pair of vertices. This can be explained by the fact that T should not contain any circuit; '

– $e = n - 1$. This result can be proved by induction:

Basis of induction:

The unit tree with $n = 1$ does not contain any edge $\begin{cases} n = 1 \\ e = 0 \end{cases}$

Thus, the equality $e = n - 1$ holds. Induction step:

Given a tree T with $e = n - 1$, if we increment the number of edges, three cases follow:

- n remains the same: the new edge links two existing vertices. The graph obtained is not a tree as it will give rise to a circuit.

- $n' \longleftarrow n + 1$: the new vertex becomes a new leaf. In the sequel, the new graph T' with n' vertices and e' edges remains a tree as $\begin{cases} T' \text{is connex} \\ e' = n' + 1 \end{cases}$

$- n \longleftarrow n + 2$: the new edge is a disconnected component, hence, the graph obtained is not connected $\Rightarrow$ It is not a tree

$$x$$

$\bullet$

Figure 1.5. *A tree T with $n = 1$*

To sum up the above proof, when adding an edge to a tree, we should add exactly one vertex.

1.6.6. *The bipartite graphs*

$-$ A graph G is said to be bipartite if the the vertex set V can be split into two separate subsets A and B such that:

- $A \cap B = \emptyset$;

- $A \cup B = V$;

- $\nexists \{x, y\} \in E | x \in A$ and $y \in B$.

A and B are disjoint sets of V such that vertices within a subset are not adjacent.

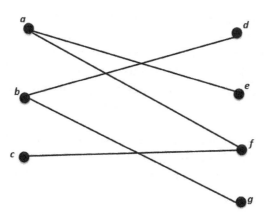

Figure 1.6. *A bipartite graph with $n = 7$ and $e = 5$*

– A complete bipartite graph connects all nodes of the first vertex set A to all nodes of the vertex set B. This yields to a total number of edges accounting to:

$$e = |A| \times |B| \qquad [1.6]$$

Bipartite graphs are used to model packing problems such as the knapsack problem, the bin packing and their variants.

1.7. Conclusion

In this chapter, we discussed various aspects of an optimization problem and the main concepts of graph theory. We addressed the key issues to consider when solving a combinatorial optimization problem. The main optimization models for the decision-making were introduced as they provide tools for making optimal and promising decisions. Indeed, optimization models are closely linked to their mathematical formulation as an objective function and a set of system constraints, and hence the definition of the feasible space. The complexity theory and the optimization methods are linked in such a way that the choice of the solution method often depends on the problem complexity. In the case of problems in class $\mathcal{P}$, a polynomial algorithm can be used. However, for $\mathcal{NP}$-hard problems, two possibilities can be adopted. While exact methods are used for finding the optimal solution for small-sized problems, approximate methods are efficient for large-size instances.

The different definitions and concepts provided in this chapter are the foundation of the theoretical and applicative contributions to be evoked in the subsequent chapters of this book.

2

Knapsack Problems

2.1. Introduction

The knapsack problem (KP) is one of the widely and extensively studied resource allocation problems. In its basic version, we are given a number of items from which we are required to select a subset to carry in a fixed capacity knapsack. Items differ by their value and their required place in the knapsack. The aim is to load items that maximize the overall reward without exceeding the capacity. The KP belongs to the class of packing problems. It is characterized by its simple structure and the ability to formulate and solve more complex optimization problems. In fact, the KP models a wide range of industrial situations belonging to the domains of transportation as cargo loading, cutting stock [GIL 66], telecommunication, reliability, advertisement, budget allocation and financial management [KAP 66].

The KP derives its name from the hiker's problem of selecting which items, among a predefined set, to fill his knapsack in such a way that the overall value of selected items is maximized such that the knapsack weight capacity is not exceeded. We address in this chapter the 0-1 KP, followed by its graph modeling, and investigate its main variants. All detailed KPs are illustrated by numerical example to show the impact of each assumption on the optimal packing solution.

2.2. Graph modeling of the knapsack problem

The KP can be defined as a bipartite graph $G = (V, E)$ such that $V = X \cup Y$ where X designates the set of items ($|X| = n$) and Y corresponds to the two alternatives: in the knapsack, out of the knapsack } $\Rightarrow |Y| = 2$.

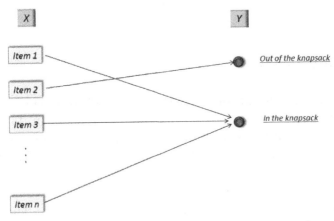

Figure 2.1. *A knapsack problem as a bipartite graph*

2.3. Notation

Following are the notations adopted in this chapter.

SYMBOLS	EXPLANATION
n	Number of items
P_i	Profit of item i
w_i	Weight of item i
W	Capacity of the knapsack
x_i	1 if item i is loaded and 0 otherwise

2.4. 0-1 knapsack problem

Necessary conditions: for the 0-1 KP, two conditions should be fulfilled:

$- \sum_{i=1}^{n} w_i \geq W$;

$- w_i \leq W, \quad i = 1, \ldots, n.$

$$
O_1 \begin{cases} p_1 \\ w_1 \end{cases} \quad O_2 \begin{cases} p_2 \\ w_2 \end{cases} \quad \ldots \quad O_n \begin{cases} p_n \\ w_n \end{cases}
$$

$\Downarrow$ *Loading*

A knapsack with capacity W

A KP consists of selecting a number of items, from a given set, to be packed in a knapsack. Each item is associated with value v_i and weight w_i, and the knapsack has a limited weight capacity W. The KP has to fill the knapsack in such a way that its content has maximum value under the capacity constraint.

The KP is mathematically stated as follows:

$$
Max \; Z(x) = \sum_{i=1}^{n} p_i x_i
$$

$S.t.$

$$
\sum_{i=1}^{n} w_i x_i \leq W
$$

$$
x_i = 0 \text{ or } 1 \qquad i = 1, \ldots, n
$$

[2.1]

The above description corresponds to the *0-1 KP*. Several variants of the basic KP were studied in the literature. In this chapter, we propose to explore three main variants that differ by generalizing the number of knapsacks, the definition of the profit and the dependance of the weight. As reported in Table 2.4, four KP variants are highlighted in this chapter. They differ in terms of the number of knapsacks to be loaded, item' weights and item' profits. KP variants pointed out in Table 2.4 are:

– the multiple KP (MKP): that extends the basic 0-1 KP by considering m knapsacks;

– the mutlidimensional KP (MDKP): in which case the weight is resource-dependent;

– the quadratic KP (QKP): that computes individual as well as joint profits for item loading;

– the quadratic multidimensional KP (QMDKP): considering both joint profits and resource-dependent weights and multiple knapsacks.

Parameter	0-1 KP	KP variant	Designation
|knapsacks|	1	m	*MKP*
Weights	w_i	a weight w_{ik} for resource k	*MDKP*
Profits	p_i	p_{ij} a joint profit for pairs of items i and j	*QKP*
(Weights, Profits)	(w_i, p_i)	(w_{ik}, p_{ij})	*QMDKP*

Table 2.1. *Some KP variants*

2.5. An example

Let's consider a 0-1 KP with $n = 7$ and a knapsack of capacity $W = 200$.

1) *Data inputs:* item profits and weights are reported in Table 1.

Item	1	2	3	4	5	6	7
Profit	20	30	15	80	5	40	10
Weight	50	30	90	70	40	120	10

Table 2.2. *Data inputs for an 0-1 KP with $n = 7$ and $W = 200$*

2) *Mathematical formulation:* the KP example is written as follows:

$$Max\ Z(x) = 20x_1 + 30x_2 + 15x_3 + 80x_4 + 5x_5 + 40x_6 + 10x_7$$
$$S.t.$$
$$50x_1 + 30x_2 + 90x_3 + 70x_4 + 40x_5 + 120x_6 + 10x_7 \leq 200 \qquad [2.2]$$
$$x_1, \dots, x_7 \in \{0, 1\}$$

3) *Optimal solution:* the resolution of the 0-1 KP yields to the optimal solution $x^* = (1, 1, 0, 1, 1, 0, 1)$. The objective function $Z(x^*) = 145$.

2.6. Multiple knapsack problem

A main variant of the 0-1 KP consists of generalizing the number of knapsacks to m with respective capacities W_j ($j = 1, \dots, m$). The MKP differs from the basic KP by the possibility of considering m knapsacks while keeping the assumption of packing a subset of items.

2.6.1. *Mathematical model*

The MKP assumptions give rise to the following mathematical model:

$$S.t.$$
$$\sum_{i=1}^{n} w_i x_{ij} \leq W_j \qquad\qquad [2.3]$$
$$\sum_{j=1}^{m} x_{ij} \leq 1, i = 1, \dots, n$$
$$x_{ij} \in \{0, 1\} \qquad\qquad i = 1, \dots, n, j = 1, \dots, m$$

The MKP tries to maximize the total profit of the selected items. Decision variables $x_{ij} \in \{0,1\}$ show whether item i is loaded in knapsack j or not. If the number of knapsacks is $m = 1$, the problem becomes a 0-1 KP.

2.6.2. *An example*

Let us consider an MKP with $n = 7$ and 2 knapsacks of capacity $C = 80$.

1) *Data inputs:* items' profits and weights are reported in Table 1.

Item	1	2	3	4	5	6	7
Profit	20	30	15	80	5	40	10
Weight	50	30	20	60	40	35	10

Table 2.3. *Data inputs for an MKP with $n = 7$ and $c_1 = c_2 = 80$*

2) The mathematical formulation of the MKP with $n = 7$, $m = 2$ and $c_j = 80$ $(j = 1, 2)$ is written as follows:

$$
\begin{aligned}
Max \ Z(x) = \ & 20x_{11} + 30x_{21} + 15x_{31} + 80x_{41} + 5x_{51} + 40x_{61} + 10x_{71} \\
& + 20x_{12} + 30x_{22} + 15x_{32} + 80x_{42} + 5x_{52} + 40x_{62} + 10x_{72}
\end{aligned}
$$

S.t.
$$
\begin{aligned}
& 50x_{11} + 30x_{21} + 20x_{31} + 60x_{41} + 40x_{51} + 35x_{61} + 10x_{71} \leq 80 \\
& 50x_{12} + 30x_{22} + 20x_{32} + 60x_{42} + 40x_{52} + 35x_{62} + 10x_{72} \leq 80 \\
& x_{11} + x_{12} \leq 1 \\
& x_{21} + x_{22} \leq 1 \\
& x_{31} + x_{32} \leq 1 \\
& x_{41} + x_{42} \leq 1 \\
& x_{51} + x_{52} \leq 1 \\
& x_{61} + x_{62} \leq 1 \\
& x_{71} + x_{72} \leq 1 \\
& x_{ij} \in \{0,1\}, \ i = 1,\ldots,7 \ \ j = 1,2
\end{aligned}
$$

[2.4]

3) The resolution of the MKP yields to the optimal solution, as reported in the screenshot in Figure 2.2, is $x^* = (0, 1, 0, 0, 0, 1, 1, 0, 0, 1, 1, 0, 0, 0)$. The objective function is $Z(x^*) = 175$. Regarding the formulation of the 0-1 KP, the

MKP needs too much structural constraints to ensure that each item can be loaded at most in one knapsack, while respecting knapsack capacity constraints.

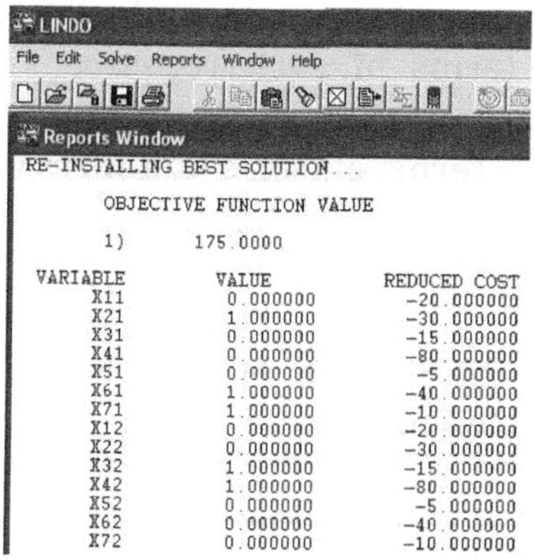

Figure 2.2. *Output of the LINDO optimizer for an MKP with $n = 7$ and $m = 2$*

2.7. Multidimensional knapsack problem

As for the MDKP, the multidimensionality of the problem consists of assuming that m resources are to be considered in the selection of items. Each item i needs an amount w_{ij} regarding resource j.

2.7.1. *Mathematical model*

This version of the KP yields to the writing of the following mathematical model:

$$
\begin{aligned}
Max \ Z(x) &= \sum_{i=1}^{n} \sum_{j=1}^{m} p_i x_{ij} \\
S.t. \quad &\sum_{i=1}^{n} w_{ik} x_{ij} \leq W_k, \quad k = 1, \ldots, r \\
&x_{ij} \in \{0, 1\} \qquad\qquad i = 1, \ldots, n, j = 1, \ldots, n
\end{aligned}
$$

[2.5]

– The objective function expresses the maximization of the total profit of selected items while checking system constraints.

– We point out r system constraints expressing the need of each item in terms of each resource k. Note that the number of knapsacks remains 1; therefore, decision variables are indexed only in terms of items' numbers (x_i, $i = 1, \ldots, n$).

2.7.2. An example

We reconsider the 0-1 KP of the basic 0-1 KP with the previously announced profits.

1) *Data inputs:*

Item	1	2	3	4	5	6	7
Profit	20	30	15	80	5	40	10

while replacing the weights w_i by the following resource-dependent w_{ik}, where the number of resources is $r = 3$. We consider following (3×7) weight-matrix W:

$$W = \begin{pmatrix} 50 & 30 & 90 & 70 & 40 & 120 & 10 \\ 12 & 5 & 38 & 6 & 23 & 10 & 35 \\ 40 & 30 & 60 & 10 & 5 & 15 & 8 \end{pmatrix}$$

2) *Mathematical formulation:* using the above mentioned input data, we obtain the following mathematical optimization problem:

$$Max\ Z(x) = 20x_1 + 30x_2 + 15x_3 + 80x_4 + 5x_5 + 40x_6 + 10x_7$$

S.t.

$$50x_1 + 30x_2 + 90x_3 + 70x_4 + 40x_5 + 120x_6 + 10x_7 \le 200$$
$$12x_1 + 5x_2 + 38x_3 + 6x_4 + 23x_5 + 10x_6 + 35x_7 \le 80$$
$$40x_1 + 30x_2 + 60x_3 + 10x_4 + 50x_5 + 150x_6 + 8x_7 \le 160$$
$$x_1, \ldots, x_7 \in \{0, 1\}$$

[2.6]

3) *The optimal solution*, as output by LINDO in Figure 2.3, is $x^* = (1, 1, 0, 1, 0, 0, 1)$ corresponding to the objective function $Z(x^*) = 140$.

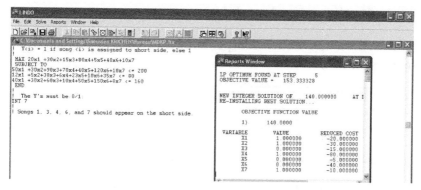

Figure 2.3. *Output of the LINDO optimizer for a MDKP*
with $n = 7$ and $r = 2$

2.8. Quadratic knapsack problem

A generalization of the 0-1 KP of great interest is related to the consideration of joint profits of loading pairs of items, named the QKP. Subsequently, profits are the summation of two main V_P and P defined as follows:

– Individual profits p_i expressed as:

$$V_P = (p_1, p_2, \ldots, p_n) \qquad [2.7]$$

– Joint profits p_{ij} generated by the loading of both items i and j. This yields to the input of a non-negative $(n \times n)$ profit matrix P defined in the following way:

$$P = \begin{pmatrix} p_{11} & p_{12} & \cdots & p_{1n} \\ p_{21} & p_{22} & \cdots & p_{2n} \\ \vdots & & \ddots & \\ p_{n1} & p_{n2} & \cdots & p_{nn} \end{pmatrix} \qquad [2.8]$$

We can note that diagonal elements p_{ii} of P correspond to the profit of loading item i in the knapsack. Hence, the individual profit c_i is already embedded in the profit matrix P.

2.8.1. *Mathematical model*

Based on the above components, the QKP is modeled as follows:

$$
\begin{aligned}
&Max\ Z(x) = \sum_{i=1}^{n} p_i x_i + \sum_{i=1}^{n} \sum_{j=i+1}^{n} p_{ij} x_i x_j \\
&S.t. \\
&\quad \sum_{i=1}^{n} w_i x_i \leq W \\
&\quad x_i \in \{0,1\}, i = 1, \ldots, n
\end{aligned}
\qquad [2.9]
$$

We can note that the mathematical formulation [2.9] is nonlinear; therefore, we can use the LINGO optimizer for solving small-sized instances. For large scaled QKPs, approximate approaches are suitable to generate effective near optimal solutions.

2.8.2. *An example*

We consider a QKP with $n = 7$ and a knapsack with capacity $W = 200$. Problem data are summarized as follows:

Item	1	2	3	4	5	6	7
Weight	50	30	90	70	40	120	10

The profit matrix P is:

$$
P = \begin{pmatrix}
20 & 10 & 30 & 0 & 50 & 0 & 90 \\
10 & 30 & 0 & 90 & 25 & 0 & 15 \\
30 & 0 & 15 & 0 & 17 & 36 & 45 \\
0 & 90 & 0 & 80 & 0 & 0 & 50 \\
50 & 25 & 17 & 0 & 5 & 9 & 65 \\
0 & 0 & 36 & 0 & 9 & 40 & 30 \\
90 & 15 & 45 & 50 & 65 & 30 & 10
\end{pmatrix}
\qquad [2.10]
$$

The formulation of the corresponding QKP is the following:

$$Max\ Z(x) = xPx = \sum_{i=1}^{7} p_i + \sum_{i=1}^{6} \sum_{j=i+1}^{7} p_{ij} x_i x_j$$

$S.t.$

$$50x_1 + 30x_2 + 90x_3 + 70x_4 + 40x_5 + 120x_6 + 10x_7 \leq 200 \qquad [2.11]$$

$$x_1, \ldots, x_7 \in \{0, 1\}$$

Where $x = (x_1\ x_2\ \ldots\ x_n)$ is a binary line vector so that the objective function $Z(x) = xPx$ is a scalar expressing the profit of selecting a subset of items in the knapsack.

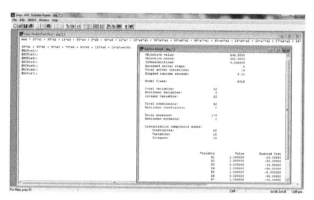

Figure 2.4. *A QKP with $n = 7$ and $W = 200$*

As reported in Figure 2.4, the optimal solution $x^* = (1, 1, 0, 1, 1, 0, 1)$ with an objective function $Z(x^*) = 540$.

2.9. Quadratic multidimensional knapsack problem

A more generalized version of the 0-1 KP consists of handling joint profits of pairs of selected items and the loading process in multiple knapsacks.

2.9.1. *Mathematical model*

This yields to the generalization of the mathematical model [2.9] to the m-knapsack case, as follows:

$$
\begin{aligned}
&Max \ Z(x) = \sum_{i=1}^{n} p_i x_i + \sum_{i=1}^{n} \sum_{j=i+1}^{n} p_{ij} x_i x_j \\
&S.t. \\
&\qquad \sum_{i=1}^{n} w_{ij} x_i \leq W_j, \quad j = 1, \ldots, r \\
&\qquad x_i \in \{0, 1\}, \ i = 1, \ldots, n
\end{aligned}
\qquad [2.12]
$$

It is understood from the statement model [2.12] that this knapsack variant supports the multidimensionality and the quadratic features.

2.9.2. *An example*

We study a QMKP proposed by Gallo *et al.* [GAL 80] with $n = 10$ items and $m = 3$ knapsacks where the profit matrix is:

$$
P = \begin{pmatrix}
9 & 86 & 0 & 0 & 0 & 0 & 0 & 31 & 0 & 0 \\
86 & 12 & 0 & 0 & 0 & 90 & 0 & 0 & 25 & 0 \\
0 & 0 & 95 & 0 & 0 & 0 & 36 & 0 & 0 & 0 \\
0 & 0 & 0 & 69 & 0 & 32 & 0 & 0 & 34 & 0 \\
0 & 0 & 0 & 0 & 27 & 0 & 0 & 0 & 0 & 0 \\
0 & 90 & 0 & 32 & 0 & 98 & 15 & 0 & 0 & 96 \\
0 & 0 & 36 & 0 & 0 & 15 & 91 & 0 & 0 & 42 \\
31 & 0 & 0 & 0 & 0 & 0 & 0 & 47 & 9 & 0 \\
0 & 25 & 0 & 34 & 0 & 0 & 0 & 9 & 41 & 98 \\
0 & 0 & 0 & 0 & 0 & 96 & 42 & 0 & 98 & 74
\end{pmatrix}
\qquad [2.13]
$$

P is symmetric so as to express, in its diagonal, individual profits of selected items and joint profits $p_{ij} = p_{ji}$ generated by the selection of both items i and j in the knapsack.

Knapsack capacities are: $W_1 = 187$, $W_2 = 190$, $W_3 = 111$. Item weights are reported in the following matrix W, where w_{ik} expresses the weight of item i according to the resource k:

$$W = \begin{pmatrix} 47 & 6 & 23 & 1 & 43 & 3 & 31 & 41 & 36 & 16 \\ 19 & 5 & 43 & 38 & 14 & 41 & 43 & 1 & 2 & 13 \\ 18 & 38 & 31 & 13 & 29 & 38 & 20 & 18 & 43 & 3 \end{pmatrix} \qquad [2.14]$$

This example is solved using LINGO, as shown in Figure 2.5. The optimizer converges to the global optimum $x^* = (0,0,1,1,0,1,1,0,0,1)$, where the objective function amounts to $Z(x^*) = 648$.

2.10. Solution approaches for knapsack problems

As KPs were extensively studied in the literature, various algorithms have been proposed including both exact and approximate approaches. While exact methods converge to optimal solutions, the computation time is costly due to the non-polynomial (NP-hardness) of the KP. Hence, for large scaled KPs, exact methods are not able to generate optimal solutions. Subsequently, approximate methods constitute the most promising recourse for solving such a class of combinatorial optimization problems. The practical and theoretical importance of the KP generated a large body of literature on both exact and approximate solution approaches. Freville and Hanafi have provided an excellent literature review on the KP and its recently developed methods.

2.10.1. *The greedy algorithm*

The most popular packing heuristic that enables 0-1 KP to be solved efficiently, giving rise to optimal or near-optimal packing solutions is based on the ranking of items according to their unit profits computed as the fraction of the profit and the weight. This ranking enables a profitable packing based on unit profits. The outline of the greedy algorithm is announced as follows:

Algorithm 1 The greedy algorithm

1: Rank items according to the decreasing order of the ratio $\frac{p_i}{w_i}$, for $i = 1, \ldots, n$

2: $W' \leftarrow W$

3: For $k = 1, \ldots, n$

4: If $w_k \leq W'$

    – Load item k of the ranked list

    – $W' \leftarrow W' - w_k$

5: end for

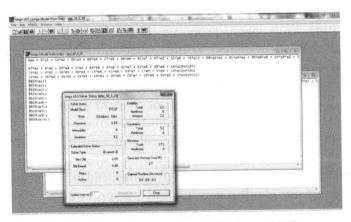

Figure 2.5. *Screenshot of LINGO for a QMKP
with $n = 10$ and $m = 3$*

2.10.2. *A genetic algorithm for the KP*

Genetic algorithms (GA) are global optimization techniques that generate promising solutions for hard-constrained optimization problems. First proposed by Holland *et al.* [HOL 92], its main characterization is the evolutionary generational process that borrows biological features. Its iterative design performs well with the resolution of the KP and its variants.

The GA starts with a set of solutions, denoted by chromosomes, to constitute an initial population. A new population is created from solutions of an old population in hope of getting a better population. Solutions which are then chosen to form new solutions (offspring) are selected according to their fitness. The more suitable the solutions, the bigger chances they have to reproduce. This process is repeated until some condition is satisfied. Most GA methods are based on the following elements: populations of chromosomes, selection according to fitness, crossover to produce new offspring and random mutation of new offspring.

2.10.2.1. *Solution encoding*

A solution to the KP can be modeled as an n-sized binary array where each position i informs whether the corresponding item i is inside or outside the knapsack. The encoding of a solution is the following:

$$\begin{array}{cccccc} 1 & 2 & 3 & \ldots & & n \\ \hline 0 & 1 & 1 & \ldots & 1 & 0 & 1 \\ \hline \end{array}$$

The above solution indicates that $item_1$ is out of the knapsack, $item_2$ and $item_3$ are in the knapsack and so on.

2.10.2.2. *Crossover*

One way for improving the solution quality of currently evaluated solutions is the use of the crossover operation that consists of combining the gene chains of two selected chromosomes to obtain new chromosomes. The crossover can be simple or multiple. Simple crossover consists of exchanging portions of the two chains in a single point while the second includes several points of crossing. For the sake of simplicity, we use the one-point crossover that selects two chromosomes, then exchange the two portions in order to get new solutions. The process can be described as follows:

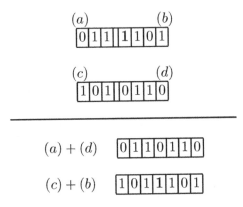

2.10.2.3. *Mutation*

The mutation operator randomly inverses two genes, corresponding to the assignment of two randomly selected items. Their reassignment can yield to an improvement of the solution.

In the above scheme, $item_2$ and $item_6$ are selected for the mutation. The exchange of the two genes makes $item_2$ out of the knapsack and $item_6$ in the knapsack.

2.11. Conclusion

We studied in this chapter the 0-1 KP and most of its variants when modifying some inputs as the number of knapsacks, the profit structure and the weight. For each problem variant, we stated its main features followed by didactic examples to learn how to operationalize an optimization model using an optimizer as LINDO. We reviewed the existing literature of the KP. As the KP is one of the most renowned and extensively studied problems in the literature, several exact and heuristic algorithms have been designed to provide concurrential solutions. We explored some approximate approaches, such as the greedy algorithm and the GA. It was proven in the existing literature that these two approaches are efficient for solving this class of optimization problems.

Algorithm 2 A genetic algorithm for the KP

1: Initialization:

- Randomly generate a population of N chromosomes
- Calculate the fitness of each chromosome

2: Create a new population:

3: Selection: Randomly select 2 chromosomes from the population.

4: Crossover: Perform crossover on the 2 chromosomes selected.

5: Mutation: Perform mutation on the chromosomes obtained.

6: Replace: Replace the current population with the new population.

7: Test: Test whether the end condition is satisfied. If so, stop. If not, return the best solution in current population and go to Step 2.

3

Packing Problems

3.1. Introduction

The bin packing problem (BPP) has attracted the attention of many researchers over the last three decades. The problem is a class of optimization problems [PAP 82] that addresses the packing of a set of items inside a set of bins so that the packing of each bin fulfills the capacity limit. One of the common objectives is the minimization of the total number of used bins or the maximization of the used space. Apart from its theoretical interest, the BPP performs well in the modeling of real-world applications in several domains such as the planning of telecommunication, transportation, production and logistics/supply-chain systems. A large variety of different bin packing applications is pointed out in [WAS 07]. Since the problem is $\mathcal{NP}$-hard [GAR 79], a great deal of works on the design and analysis of heuristics [COF 97] and few handful of papers have been devoted to the computation of lower bounds and the design of exact algorithms [MAR 90b, LAB 95, BOU 05]. Throughout this chapter, we present the most recent results for bin packing and other related problems focusing on the writing of the mathematical models. Many extensions and generalizations of the basic BPP can be identified in the literature. The vector packing problem (VPP) considers items characterized by their sizes in several dimensions, and the bins have a limited size in each dimension. This problem is thoroughly discussed in [KEL 04]. Another problem that is considered as the dual of the BPP is the scheduling on parallel machine problem. An overview of these problems is presented in this chapter. As the solution approaches, we present specific approximate methods and a genetic algorithm (GA) metaheuristic. Approximate methods from the literature are generally greedy algorithms based on simple procedures. For the genetic algorithm, we showed that numerous encodings are of interest.

3.2. Graph modeling of the bin packing problem

The BPP can be defined as a bipartite graph $G = (V, E)$ such that V is split on two disjoint sets $V = X \cup Y$ where X is the set of items ($|X| = n$) and Y corresponds to the set of bins ($|Y| = m$).

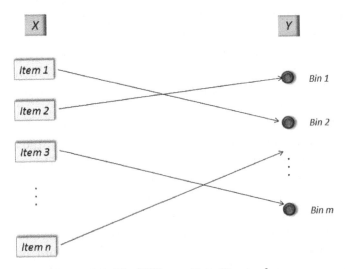

Figure 3.1. *The BPP as a bipartite graph*

3.3. Notation

The following notations are adopted for the basic BPP.

Symbols	Explanations
N	Set of items
n	Number of items
W	Bin capacity
V	Set of items
$i,\ k$	Indices of items and bins, respectively
w_i	Weight of item i
$G(V, E)$	Conflicts graph of V vertex and E edges
$Z(x)$	The objective function to be optimized

3.4. Basic bin packing problem

The BPP deals with packing a set of $N = \{1, 2, \ldots, n\}$ items into identical bins. Each item has a specified size or weight w_i $(i = 1, \ldots, n)$, and all bins have the same capacity c. The main objective is to find the minimum number of bins required to pack the considered set of items without violating the capacity constraints of each bin. Two objective versions of BPP can be distinguished in the literature:

– minimize the number of bins used;

– minimize the capacity W for a given number of bins m.

While in the basic version of the BPP, the number of used bins has to be minimized, the second version of the problem is equivalent to the scheduling problem that consists of assigning n jobs, each having a processing time p_i $(i = 1, \ldots, n)$ to m identical parallel machines so that the maximum completion time of jobs makespan c is minimized [CHE 90]. Note that both of the problem versions are NP-hard in the strong sense [GAR 79] and are based on the decision problem of finding a feasible solution for a given combination of c and m. Kantorovich [KAN 60] introduced the first model for a cutting-stock problem based on integer linear programming.

3.4.1. *Mathematical modeling of the BPP*

The following model tends to minimize the number of used bins for feasible packing solutions.

$$
\begin{aligned}
&Min \ Z(x) = \sum_{j=1}^{n} y_j \\
&S.t. \\
&\quad \sum_{i=1}^{n} w_{ij} x_{ij} \leq W y_j, \ j = 1, \ldots, m \\
&\quad \sum_{j=1}^{m} x_{ij} = 1, \ i = 1, \ldots, n \\
&\quad x_{ij} \in \{0, 1\}, \ i = 1, \ldots, n, \ j = 1, \ldots, m \\
&\quad y_j \in \{0, 1\}, \ j = 1, \ldots, m
\end{aligned}
\tag{3.1}
$$

– The objective function of the optimization model (3.1) consists of minimizing the number of bins used.

– The first set of constraints expresses the weight capacity limit, for each bin, to be fulfilled. Note that the right-hand side of each inequality obliges y_j to take the value 1 whenever an item i is assigned to bin j.

– The second set of constraints of model [3.1] imposes that each item is packed in exactly one bin.

– y_j is a binary variable that takes 1 if bin j is used, 0 otherwise. The binary variable x_{ij} takes 1 if item i is placed in bin j, 0 otherwise.

Any solution that respects the previously stated packing requirements is a feasible solution. It is worth mentioning that such formulation can be solved either using an exact method or heuristically, using a specific heuristic or a metaheuristic approach. As the problem is NP-hard, we propose to illustrate the optimization problem [3.1] by a small-scaled BPP that counts $n = 7$ items, then develop for large-sized BPPs the most used heuristics and an adapted GA to accurately approximate the optimal solution.

3.4.2. *An example*

Let us consider a BPP with $n = 7$ and a number of identical bins $m = 4$ with capacities $W = 200$. Each item i is characterized by its weight w_i, recorded in Table 3.6.2.

Item	1	2	3	4	5	6	7
Weight	50	30	90	70	40	120	10

Table 3.1. *Data inputs for a BPP with $n = 7$ and $W = 200$*

The mathematical formulation of the problem is written as follows:

$$Max\ Z(x) = y_1 + y_2 + y_3 + y_4$$
$$S.t.$$
$$50x_1 + 30x_2 + 90x_3 + 70x_4 + 40x_5 + 120x_6 + 10x_7 \leq 200y_1$$
$$50x_1 + 30x_2 + 90x_3 + 70x_4 + 40x_5 + 120x_6 + 10x_7 \leq 200y_2$$
$$50x_1 + 30x_2 + 90x_3 + 70x_4 + 40x_5 + 120x_6 + 10x_7 \leq 200y_3$$
$$50x_1 + 30x_2 + 90x_3 + 70x_4 + 40x_5 + 120x_6 + 10x_7 \leq 200y_4$$
$$x_{11} + x_{12} + x_{13} + x_{14} = 1$$
$$x_{21} + x_{22} + x_{23} + x_{24} = 1 \hspace{2cm} [3.2]$$
$$x_{31} + x_{32} + x_{33} + x_{34} = 1$$
$$x_{41} + x_{42} + x_{43} + x_{44} = 1$$
$$x_{51} + x_{52} + x_{53} + x_{54} = 1$$
$$x_{61} + x_{62} + x_{63} + x_{64} = 1$$
$$x_{71} + x_{72} + x_{73} + x_{74} = 1$$
$$y_1, \ldots, y_7 \in \{0, 1\}$$
$$x_{ij} \in \{0, 1\}, \quad i = 1, \ldots, 7 \quad j = 1, \ldots, 4$$

3.5. Variable cost and size BPP

The variable cost and size BPP (VCSBPP) is a generalization of the basic BPP where it is assumed that the bins do not have identical capacities or packing costs. It consists of packing a set of items into a set of bins so that the bins' capacities are respected and the total cost associated with the packing configuration is minimized. Following are the additional notations to be redefined:

Symbols	Explanations
n	Number of items
c_j	Packing cost in bin j
V_j	Capacity of bin j
v_i	Volume of item i

3.5.1. *Mathematical model*

The mathematical model of the VCSBPP is expressed in the following way:

$$Min\ Z(x) = \sum_{j=1}^{n} \sum_{k=1}^{m} c_j y_j$$
$$S.t.$$
$$\sum_{i=1}^{n} v_i x_{ij} \leq V_j y_j, \ j = 1, \ldots, m$$
$$\sum_{j=1}^{m} x_{ij} = 1, \ i = 1, \ldots, n$$
$$x_{ij} \in \{0, 1\}, \ i = 1, \ldots, n, \ j = 1, \ldots, m$$
$$y_j \in \{0, 1\}, \ j = 1, \ldots, m$$

[3.3]

The objective function of the model [3.3] minimizes the cost of the used bins for the packing of items. The first set of constraints ensures that packed items in each bin do not exceed their volume V_j. The second set of constraints makes sure that each item is packed in exactly one bin.

3.5.2. An example

We consider a VCSBPP with $n = 7$ items and $m = 4$ bins where each item is characterized by its volume and each bin by its cost. The data inputs of the problem are reported in the following:

Number	1	2	3	4	5	6	7
Item volumes	50	30	90	70	40	120	10
Bin costs	200	150	30	500	–	–	–
Bin volumes	100	200	70	250	–	–	–

The corresponding optimization problem is written:

$$Min \ Z(x) = 200y_1 + 150y_2 + 30y_3 + 500y_4$$
$$S.t.$$

$$50x_1 + 30x_2 + 90x_3 + 70x_4 + 40x_5 + 120x_6 + 10x_7 \leq 100y_1$$
$$50x_1 + 30x_2 + 90x_3 + 70x_4 + 40x_5 + 120x_6 + 10x_7 \leq 200y_2$$
$$50x_1 + 30x_2 + 90x_3 + 70x_4 + 40x_5 + 120x_6 + 10x_7 \leq 70y_3$$
$$50x_1 + 30x_2 + 90x_3 + 70x_4 + 40x_5 + 120x_6 + 10x_7 \leq 250y_4$$
$$x_{11} + x_{12} + x_{13} + x_{14} = 1$$
$$x_{21} + x_{22} + x_{23} + x_{24} = 1 \qquad\qquad [3.4]$$
$$x_{31} + x_{32} + x_{33} + x_{34} = 1$$
$$x_{41} + x_{42} + x_{43} + x_{44} = 1$$
$$x_{51} + x_{52} + x_{53} + x_{54} = 1$$
$$x_{61} + x_{62} + x_{63} + x_{64} = 1$$
$$x_{71} + x_{72} + x_{73} + x_{74} = 1$$
$$y_1, \ldots, y_7 \in \{0, 1\}$$
$$x_{ij} \in \{0, 1\}, \quad i = 1, \ldots, 7 \ \ j = 1, \ldots, 4$$

3.6. Vector BPP

The basic BPP considers, in the packing of items, only item weights. However, under some circumstances, it is worth mentioning that other item features such as the length, width and the height introduced by Garey et al. [GAR 76] should be taken into account. This version of the BPP, called the d-dimensional vector packing problem (d-DVPP), has applications in loading, scheduling and layout design. The objective is to pack the items into a minimum number of bins while respecting the capacity constraints of each dimension d. It is worth mentioning that in the d-DVPP each dimension is independent of the others. Hence, this problem is different from the d-dimensional BPP where hyper-rectangles have to be packed into hypercubes [CHA 93]. The d-DVPP arises in a large variety of real-world applications such as computer science, production planning and logistics. In [PAN 11], the authors describe the efficiency of the d-DVPP in modeling resource allocation problem and especially the virtual machine placement problem. Another application of the d-DVPP in packing steel products is presented in [CHA 05]. As part of this chapter, we focus on the two-dimensional vector packing problem (2-DVPP) [SPI 94] which is a special case of the d-DVPP arising when $d = 2$. The problem deals with packing a set of $N = \{1, \ldots, n\}$ items, each having, say, a weight w_i and a length l_i, and $M = \{1, \ldots, m\}$ identical bins with weight and length capacities W and L, respectively, into the minimum number of bins and without violating the capacity constraints.

3.6.1. *Mathematical model*

An integer linear programming for the 2-DVPP can be stated as follows:

$$Min\ Z(x) = \sum_{j=1}^{n} y_j$$

S.t.

$$\sum_{i=1}^{n} w_{ij} x_{ij} \leq W y_j,\ j = 1, \ldots, m$$
$$\sum_{j=1}^{m} x_{ij} = 1,\ i = 1, \ldots, n$$
$$\sum_{i=1}^{n} l_i x_{ij} \leq L y_j,\ j = 1, \ldots, m$$
$$x_{ij} \in \{0, 1\},\quad i = 1, \ldots, n,\ j = 1, \ldots, m$$
$$y_j \in \{0, 1\},\quad j = 1, \ldots, m$$

[3.5]

3.6.2. *An example*

We reconsider the input data of the basic bin packing example presented in section 3.4, which are extended to support both the weight and length of the items addressed.

Item	1	2	3	4	5	6	7
Weight	50	30	90	70	40	120	10
Length	10	5	30	15	20	40	4

Table 3.2. *Data inputs for a VPP with $n = 7$ and $W = 200$*

Volume constraints that are appended in the formulation [3.2] are extended by

$$
\begin{aligned}
&Max\ Z(x) = y_1 + y_2 + y_3 + y_4 \\
&S.t. \\
&\quad 50x_1 + 30x_2 + 90x_3 + 70x_4 + 40x_5 + 120x_6 + 10x_7 \le 200y_1 \\
&\quad 50x_1 + 30x_2 + 90x_3 + 70x_4 + 40x_5 + 120x_6 + 10x_7 \le 200y_2 \\
&\quad 50x_1 + 30x_2 + 90x_3 + 70x_4 + 40x_5 + 120x_6 + 10x_7 \le 200y_3 \\
&\quad 50x_1 + 30x_2 + 90x_3 + 70x_4 + 40x_5 + 120x_6 + 10x_7 \le 200y_4 \\
&\quad x_{11} + x_{12} + x_{13} + x_{14} = 1 \\
&\quad x_{21} + x_{22} + x_{23} + x_{24} = 1 \\
&\quad x_{31} + x_{32} + x_{33} + x_{34} = 1 \\
&\quad x_{41} + x_{42} + x_{43} + x_{44} = 1 \\
&\quad x_{51} + x_{52} + x_{53} + x_{54} = 1 \\
&\quad x_{61} + x_{62} + x_{63} + x_{64} = 1 \\
&\quad x_{71} + x_{72} + x_{73} + x_{74} = 1 \\
&\quad y_1, \ldots, y_7 \in \{0,1\} \\
&\quad x_{ij} \in \{0,1\}, \ i = 1, \ldots, 7 \ j = 1, \ldots, 4
\end{aligned}
$$

[3.6]

3.7. BPP with conflicts

Formally, the BPP with conflicts (BPPCs) can be described as follows. We are given m identical bins of capacity W, a set of items $N = \{1, \ldots, n\}$ characterized by a non-negative weight $w_i \in W$, and a conflict graph $G = (V, E)$, where E is the set of edges such that $(i, j) \in E$ when i and j are in conflict. The problem is to assign items to bins, using a minimum number of bins, while ensuring that the total weight of the items assigned to a bin does not exceed the bin capacity W, and that no two items that are in conflict are assigned to the same bin. The number K is assumed to be large enough to guarantee feasibility; more precisely, it is a valid upper bound on the number of bins in an optimal solution (note that $m \leq n$). A natural and compact integer programming formulation makes use of binary variables x_{ik} taking value 1 if item i is assigned to bin k and 0 otherwise, and binary variables y_k taking value 1 if bin k is used and 0 otherwise.

3.7.1. Mathematical model

The problem is stated as follows:

$$Min\ Z(x) = \sum_{j=1}^{n} y_j$$
$$S.t.$$
$$\sum_{i=1}^{n} w_{ij} x_{ij} \leq W y_j, \ j = 1, \ldots, m$$
$$\sum_{j=1}^{m} x_{ij} = 1, \ i = 1, \ldots, n$$
$$x_{ij} + x_{kj} \leq y_j, \ \{i, j\} \in E, \ j = 1, \ldots, m \qquad [3.7]$$
$$x_{ij} \in \{0, 1\}, \ i = 1, \ldots, n, \ j = 1, \ldots, m$$
$$y_j \in \{0, 1\}, \ j = 1, \ldots, m$$

– The objective of the BPPC [3.7] remains the minimization of the number of used bins for the packing of the whole set of items.

– The first set of constraints in problem [3.7] requires that each bin capacity should be respected.

– The second set of constraints enforces the packing of each item to exactly one bin.

– The third set of constraints in the formulation [3.7] expresses the conflicts between pairs of items.

3.7.2. An example

We input in the example of section 3.4 conflicts between the following pairs of items:

1) *Data inputs:*

- $item_1$ and $item_5$;

- $item_2$ and $item_4$.

Note that, for each conflict, $m = 4$ constraints are to be written to forbid the packing of both items into the same bin. We remind the readers that the input data are reported in Table 1.

Item	1	2	3	4	5	6	7
Weight	50	30	90	70	40	120	10
Length	10	5	30	15	20	40	4

Table 3.3. *Data inputs for a VPP with* $n = 7$ *and* $W = 200$

2) *Mathematical formulation:* The following mathematical models correspond to the BPPC, where $n = 7$ items are to be packed, such that the two pairs of items $\{1, 5\}$ and $\{2, 4\}$ are in conflict:

$Max\ Z(x) = y_1 + y_2 + y_3 + y_4$

$S.t.$

$$50x_1 + 30x_2 + 90x_3 + 70x_4 + 40x_5 + 120x_6 + 10x_7 \leq 200y_1$$
$$50x_1 + 30x_2 + 90x_3 + 70x_4 + 40x_5 + 120x_6 + 10x_7 \leq 200y_2$$
$$50x_1 + 30x_2 + 90x_3 + 70x_4 + 40x_5 + 120x_6 + 10x_7 \leq 200y_3$$
$$50x_1 + 30x_2 + 90x_3 + 70x_4 + 40x_5 + 120x_6 + 10x_7 \leq 200y_4$$
$$x_{11} + x_{12} + x_{13} + x_{14} = 1$$
$$x_{21} + x_{22} + x_{23} + x_{24} = 1$$
$$x_{31} + x_{32} + x_{33} + x_{34} = 1$$
$$x_{41} + x_{42} + x_{43} + x_{44} = 1$$
$$x_{51} + x_{52} + x_{53} + x_{54} = 1$$
$$x_{61} + x_{62} + x_{63} + x_{64} = 1$$
$$x_{71} + x_{72} + x_{73} + x_{74} = 1$$
$$x_{11} + x_{51} \leq y_1$$
$$x_{12} + x_{52} \leq y_2$$
$$x_{13} + x_{53} \leq y_3$$
$$x_{14} + x_{54} \leq y_4$$
$$x_{21} + x_{41} \leq y_1$$
$$x_{22} + x_{42} \leq y_2$$
$$x_{23} + x_{43} \leq y_3$$
$$x_{24} + x_{44} \leq y_4$$
$$y_1, \ldots, y_7 \in \{0, 1\}$$
$$x_{ij} \in \{0, 1\}, \quad i = 1, \ldots, 7 \ j = 1, \ldots, 4$$

[3.8]

3.8. Solution approaches for the BPP

3.8.1. *The next-fit strategy*

In the next-fit (NF) strategy, the first item is packed into bin 1. Each further item is packed into the same bin as the preceding item, if the residual capacity of the bin is sufficient. Otherwise, it is packed into a new bin. The online version of NF has time complexity $O(n)$, whereas the offline version of next-fit-decreasing (NFD) takes time $O(n \log n)$ due to the sorting of items. Algorithm 3 outlines the NF strategy.

Algorithm 3 The next-fit template

1: Inputs A list of items $\sigma = (1, \ldots, n)$, a bin capacity C
2: Output A packing solution
3: Open a new bin j
4: For$i \leftarrow 1$ to n
5: While Existing bins
6: Pack item i into the partially filled bin
7: Update the load into the current bin
8: Pack item i into a new bin

3.8.2. *The first-fit strategy*

At each step of the first-fit (FF) strategy, the current item is assigned to the (partially filled) bin with the smallest index that has sufficient residual capacity. If no such bin is available, the item is packed into a new bin. The online version of FF takes time $O(n \log n)$ if a special data structure is used for storing the residual capacities of the bins. The offline version, first-fit-decreasing (FFD), has the same time complexity. Obviously, FF and FFD always find solutions at least as good as those found by the NF and NFD, respectively. Algorithm 4 outlines the FF strategy.

Algorithm 4 The first-fit template

1: Inputs: A list of items $\sigma = (1, \ldots, n)$, a bin capacity C
2: Output A packing solution
3: Open a new bin j
4: For $i \leftarrow 1$ To n
5: While Existing bins Pack item i into the partially filled bin with the smallest index which has sufficient residual capacity
6: If Packed Update the load into the current bin Pack item i into a new bin

---

3.8.3. *The best-fit strategy*

At each step of the best-fit (BF) strategy, the current item is assigned to the partially filled bin that has the smallest sufficient residual capacity. Ties are broken in favor of the bin with the smallest index. In the absence of such a bin, a new one is opened. The time complexity of the online version of BF and the offline version of best-fit-decreasing (BFD) is $O(n \log n)$. Algorithm 5 outlines the BF strategy.

Algorithm 5 The best-fit template

1: Inputs A list of items $\sigma = (1, \ldots, n)$, a bin capacity C
2: Output A packing solution
3: Open a new bin j
4: For $i \leftarrow 1$ to n
5: While Existing bins Pack item i into the partially filled bin which has the smallest residual capacity Ties are broken in favor of the bin with the smallest index
6: If Packed Update the load into the current binPack item i into a new bin

---

3.8.4. *The minimum bin slack*

The minimum bin slack (MBS) heuristic is a bin-focused procedure. At each step, an attempt is made to find a set of items (packing) that fits the bin capacity as much as possible.

At each stage, a list Z' of n' items not assigned to bins so far is sorted in the non-increasing order of sizes. Each time a packing is determined, the items involved are placed into a bin and removed from Z', preserving the sorting order. The process ends when the list becomes empty.

Each packing is determined in a search procedure that tests all possible subsets of items on the list which fit the bin capacity. The subset that leaves the minimal slack is adopted. If the algorithm finds a subset that completely fills up the bin, the search is stopped. The search is started from the items of a greater size (i.e. from the beginning of Z') and it is stopped when the algorithm finds a subset that fills up the bin completely. A recursive implementation is shown in algorithm 6. The procedure is launched with $q = 1$ and $A = A^* = \emptyset$, where q is the index of the item in Z' from which the processing begins, A is the set of items currently assigned to the packing and A^* is the set of items in the best packing. The slack in packing A is expressed by $s(A)$, and the number of items in Z' is denoted by n'. Clearly, $s(A)$ can be simply computed by beginning from $s(A) = c$ and updating every time an item is added to or removed from A.

Algorithm 6 The MBSOnePackingSearch(q) template

1: Inputs A list Z' of n' m, C, N, t_i
2: Output a packing solution
3: Sort Z' in a non-increasing order of sizes t_i
4: For $r \leftarrow q$ to n'
5: $i \leftarrow Z'_r$
6: If $t_i \leq s(A)$
7: $A \leftarrow A \cup \{i\}$
8: MBSOnePackingSearch(r+1)
9: $A \leftarrow A \setminus \{i\}$
10: If $s(A^*) = 0$
11: Exit
12: If $s(A) < s(A^*)$ $A^* \leftarrow A$

The time complexity of the MBS algorithm is exponential and requires $O(2^n)$. The authors proved that MBS is better, in terms of solution quality, than the FFD and BFD algorithms. It also finds an optimal solution for problem instances for which a two-bin solution exists.

3.8.5. *The minimum bin slack'*

This method is a slightly modified version of the MBS algorithm. The only difference between the MBS and the minimum bin slack' (MBS') is that at each stage an item (called seed) is chosen and permanently fixed in the resulting packing. They used the item of largest size as seed, (i.e. the first element in the list). By this modification, the authors tried to minimize the space in the bin to fill up during the search and to reduce the processing time. By comparing it with the MBS, they observed that MBS' is faster and provides superior results on average.

3.8.6. *The least loaded heuristic*

The least loaded (LL) algorithm attempts to balance the load between the bins by assigning the incoming items to the LL bin (i.e. the largest residual capacity). Starting from the item (1), try to iteratively pack item (i) into the current m bins by choosing the LL one each time. If LL fails to pack an existing item into the current m bins, it starts repacking after a new bin is opened. The process is stopped when there are no more items to pack. The template of LL is described in algorithm 3.7.

Algorithm 7 The least loaded template for the BPP

1: *Inputs:*

  − A permutation items $\sigma = (1, \ldots, n)$

  − A set of bins {1,...,m}

  − Identical bins' capacities C.

2: *Output:* A packing solution Start loading according to the lower bound of bins; for i 1 to n do while Existing bins do try to pack item i into the least loaded bin; end if Packed then Update the load into the current bin; else Pack item i into a new bin; end end

---

The heuristic can be viewed as the well-known approximating algorithm local search (LS) for the P | | Cmax (see section 2.4.3). In order to adapt LL to our 2D problem, we examine various sorting rules such as the decreasing order of their weight c_i, height h_i and $max\ c_i, h_i$. After some preliminary experiments, the most effective sorting rule is to consider the items according to a decreasing order of their height hi. In the iterative process, we choose the bin with the minimum total height among the m current bins while respecting the weight capacity constraint [3.3].

3.8.7. A genetic algorithm for the bin packing problem

3.8.7.1. Solution encoding

We point out two encoding policies [DAH 13] for a packing solution:

1) Direct encoding that consists of generating an n-sized array in which the position designates the item number and its content records the corresponding bin. Hence, the graphical illustration of the direct encoding is reported.

2) Indirect encoding is based on a permutation $\sigma = (\sigma(1), \ldots, \sigma(n))$ of n items. The major asset of these indirect approaches is that there is no need for a penalty function as only feasible solutions are generated. All the problem-specific knowledge is handled by the decoder, which is generally a greedy heuristic as the LL heuristic. As the objective is to minimize the number of bins, a decoder is applied to generate the corresponding solution. The last position of the permutation indicates the lower bound of the number of bins to be used in the decoding of the permutation.

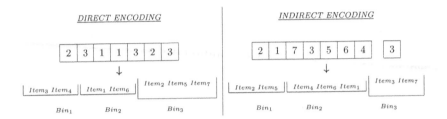

3.8.7.2. *Crossover*

The two-point crossover is generally applied for generating new offspring, once two chromosomes are selected in the population currently studied. We use the two-point crossover proposed in [ISH 98]. A pair of crossing points is randomly selected. The offspring generated preserves the items outside the two points selected from the first parent chromosome. The remaining items are inserted from the second parents while respecting the order of their appearance.

3.8.7.3. *Mutation*

Two mutation operators can be adopted, namely:

– *Shift mutation:* a pair of randomly choosing components are shifted from the permutation part of the chromosome. The lb parameter is changed by removing a random number from the old values in the chromosome.

– *Swap mutation:* a pair of randomly choosing components are swapped from the permutation part of the chromosome. The lb is changed by adding a random number to the old values in the chromosome.

3.9. Conclusion

We introduced in this chapter the BPP and some of its variants. First, a detailed statement of the basic BPP is stated, followed by its mathematical model, and an illustrative example showing its resolution using an optimizer. Next, we focused on its related problems and extensions. Despite the vast literature on such generalization, we enumerated the two main extensions of the basic BPP, namely the VCSBPP, the VPP and the BPPCs. For each problem, we stated its mathematical formulation followed by a didactic example to explain in more detail how it operates. As the BPP and its variants are NP-hard, large-sized instances cannot be solved using exact approaches within a reasonable computation time; therefore, we develop some specifically designed heuristics that output a good quality solution in a brief running time. Such solutions can also be one of the inputs in the initial population of a GA. A general outline of the GA is provided and can constitute a challenging research field that provides promising solutions for the BPP and its variants.

Algorithm 8 A genetic algorithm for the BPP

1: **Initialization:**

    – Generate an initial population of N chromosomes by applying some heuristics, as FFD or MBS, and a random generation.

    – Calculate the fitness of each chromosome

2: **Iterative process:**

    – Create a new population by applying the following operators:

      - *Selection:* Select the two elitist chromosomes from the current population.

      - *Crossover:* Perform the two-point crossover on the selected chromosomes.

      - *Mutation:* Choose randomly an item and change its bin packing regarding the slack capacity of used bins.

    – *Replacement:* Refine the new population

    – *Test:* Check the stopping rule

4

Assignment Problem

4.1. Introduction

The assignment problem (AP) is a challenging optimization problem that has the potential to model a wide variety of practical situations as network management, production planning and location area planning in telecommunication. This classical operations research model deals with the saving cost assignment of a number of tasks to a group of agents.

The general assignment problem (GAP) consists of finding the optimal assignment of n items (tasks) into m knapsacks (agents) without exceeding the capacity of any knapsack. It is required to perform all tasks by assigning exactly one agent to each task in such a way that the total cost of the assignment is minimized.

There exist many combinatorial optimization problems which have the same structure as the GAP. It is noticeable that the basic assignment structure is present in several combinatorial optimization problems such as the GAP, the timetabling problem, the graph coloring problem and the graph partitioning problem, so the GAP can be considered as a generalization of the AP.

The GAP is known to be *NP*-hard, however the problem of finding a feasible assignment is *NP*-complete.

More recently, a lot of research has been published on this popular combinatorial optimization problem. A general overview of heuristic and metaheuristic approaches for the GAP was summarized by [ÖNC 07].

We propose, in the remainder of this chapter, an exploration of some variants of the AP that differ in terms of the input parameters as the assignment that can necessitate a weight of the possibility of assigning more than one agent to each job. For each AP variant, we state its mathematical formulation and show the main difference with the basic PP. Greedy-based and GA approaches are also adapted in the last part of the chapter.

4.2. Graph modeling of the assignment problem

The AP can be defined as a bipartite graph $G = (V, E)$ such that V is split into two disjoint sets $V = X \cup Y$ where X designates the set of agents ($|X| = n$) and Y corresponds to the set of jobs ($|Y| = n$). The corresponding bipartite graph connects each agent to exactly one job.

4.3. Notation

We enumerate in what follows the main symbols used for the modeling of the AP and its variants:

SYMBOLS	*EXPLANATION*
Symbols	Explanations
n	Number of agents
C	Square cost matrix of order n
c_{ij}	Cost of assigning agent i to job j
x_{ij}	A binary decision variable that indicates whether agent i is assigned to job j

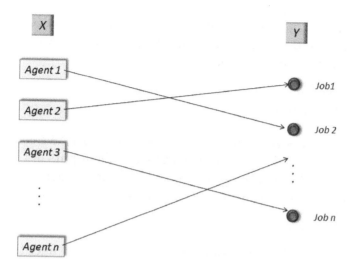

Figure 4.1. *The AP as a bipartite graph*

4.4. Mathematical formulation of the basic AP

The mathematical formulation of the AP is written as follows:

$$Min\ Z(x) = \sum_{i=1}^{m} \sum_{j=1}^{n} c_{ij}x_{ij}$$
$$S.t.$$
$$\sum_{j=1}^{n} x_{ij} = 1,\ i = 1,\ldots,n \qquad [4.1]$$
$$\sum_{i=1}^{n} x_{ij} = 1,\ j = 1,\ldots,n$$
$$x_{ij} \in \{1,0\}\quad \forall i,j$$

– The objective function of the mathematical model [4.1] refers to the minimization of the total assignment cost of agents to jobs.

– The first set of constraints of the model [4.1] define the requirement to assign exactly one agent to each job.

– The second set of constraints of the optimization problem [4.1] ensure that each job is managed by exactly one agent.

– Binary decision variables $\{x_{ij}\}$, that constitute the output, once the optimization problem is solved, represent the assignment of agent i to job j.

4.4.1. *An example*

To well illustrate the optimization model [4.1], we consider an AP with n = 7. First, we need to state the inputs of the AP, then write the mathematical model in order to generate the optimal solution using LINDO optimizer.

1) *Data inputs:*

a) $n = 7$ corresponds to the number of agents and number of jobs.

b) The cost matrix $C_{(7 \times 7)}$ is written as follows:

$$C = \begin{pmatrix} 10 & 20 & 100 & 3 & 70 & 90 & 25 \\ 60 & 50 & 40 & 10 & 200 & 300 & 30 \\ 150 & 200 & 30 & 70 & 500 & 100 & 50 \\ 10 & 12 & 400 & 30 & 90 & 100 & 230 \\ 19 & 30 & 40 & 300 & 120 & 40 & 50 \\ 45 & 25 & 70 & 100 & 150 & 11 & 400 \\ 500 & 20 & 30 & 50 & 300 & 130 & 350 \end{pmatrix}$$

2) *Mathematical formulation:*

$$\begin{aligned} Max \ Z(x) = \ &10x_{11} + 20x_{12} + 100x_{13} + 3x_{14} + 70x_{15} + 90x_{16} + 25x_{17} \\ &60x_{21} + 50x_{22} + 40x_{23} + 10x_{24} + 200x_{25} + 300x_{26} + 30x_{27} \\ &150x_{31} + 200x_{32} + 30x_{33} + 70x_{34} + 500x_{35} + 100x_{36} + 50x_{37} \\ &10x_{41} + 12x_{42} + 400x_{43} + 30x_{44} + 90x_{45} + 100x_{46} + 230x_{47} \\ &19x_{51} + 30x_{52} + 40x_{53} + 300x_{54} + 120x_{55} + 40x_{56} + 50x_{57} \\ &45x_{61} + 25x_{62} + 70x_{63} + 100x_{64} + 150x_{65} + 11x_{66} + 400x_{67} \\ &500x_{71} + 20x_{72} + 30x_{73} + 50x_{74} + 300x_{75} + 130x_{76} + 350x_{77} \end{aligned}$$

S.t.

$$x_{11} + x_{12} + x_{13} + x_{14} + x_{15} + x_{16} + x_{17} = 1$$
$$x_{21} + x_{22} + x_{23} + x_{24} + x_{25} + x_{26} + x_{27} = 1$$
$$x_{31} + x_{32} + x_{33} + x_{34} + x_{35} + x_{36} + x_{37} = 1$$
$$x_{41} + x_{42} + x_{43} + x_{44} + x_{45} + x_{46} + x_{47} = 1$$
$$x_{51} + x_{52} + x_{53} + x_{54} + x_{55} + x_{56} + x_{57} = 1$$
$$x_{61} + x_{62} + x_{63} + x_{64} + x_{65} + x_{66} + x_{67} = 1$$
$$x_{71} + x_{72} + x_{73} + x_{74} + x_{75} + x_{76} + x_{77} = 1$$
$$x_{11} + x_{21} + x_{31} + x_{41} + x_{51} + x_{61} + x_{71} = 1$$
$$x_{12} + x_{22} + x_{32} + x_{42} + x_{52} + x_{62} + x_{72} = 1$$
$$x_{13} + x_{23} + x_{33} + x_{43} + x_{53} + x_{63} + x_{73} = 1$$
$$x_{14} + x_{24} + x_{34} + x_{44} + x_{54} + x_{64} + x_{74} = 1$$
$$x_{15} + x_{25} + x_{35} + x_{45} + x_{55} + x_{65} + x_{75} = 1$$
$$x_{16} + x_{26} + x_{36} + x_{46} + x_{56} + x_{66} + x_{76} = 1$$
$$x_{17} + x_{27} + x_{37} + x_{47} + x_{575} + x_{76} + x_{77} = 1$$
$$x_{ij} \in \{0,1\}, \quad i = 1, \dots, 7 \quad j = 1, \dots, 7$$

[4.2]

3) *Optimal solution:* the output of the LINDO optimizer is reported in Figure 4.2 showing that the optimal solution x obtained after 19 iterations amounts to $Z(x) = 2750$.

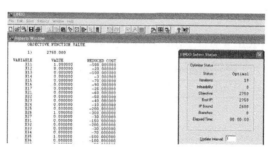

Figure 4.2. *Optimal solution by LINDO for an AP with $n = 7$*

4.5. Generalized assignment problem

The generalized assignment problem (GDAP) introduces two additional input parameters, namely the profit p_{ij} and weight w_{ij} for each agent i, once assigned to job j. Indeed, it is assumed that each job disposes of a capacity limit W_j. It consists of assigning n agents to m jobs so that the total profit generated by the assignment process is maximized. The assignment is designed in such a way that the amount of resource needed for assigning agents to each job does not exceed its available resource W_j. This generalization of the AP can be viewed as a knapsack problem.

The above announcements yield to the following optimization model:

$$
\begin{aligned}
&Max\ Z(x) = \sum_{i=1}^{n} \sum_{j=1}^{m} p_{ij} x_{ij} \\
&S.t. \\
&\quad \sum_{i=1}^{n} w_{ij} x_{ij} \leq W_j \qquad j = 1, \ldots, m \\
&\quad \sum_{j=1}^{m} x_{ij} = 1 \qquad\quad i = 1, \ldots, n
\end{aligned}
\qquad [4.3]
$$

4.5.1. *An example*

To well illustrate the GAP, we assume that the number of agents is $n = 7$ and the number of jobs is $m = 4$. The problem data and solution are reported as follows:

1) *Data inputs:*

a) Problem's size and resource amounts:

Parameter	n	m	W_1	W_2	W_3	W_4
Value	7	4	100	150	70	90

b) Profit matrix: $P_{(7 \times 4)} = \begin{pmatrix} 10 & 40 & 5 & 100 \\ 60 & 10 & 200 & 50 \\ 30 & 150 & 90 & 15 \\ 2 & 48 & 120 & 80 \\ 15 & 30 & 60 & 100 \\ 5 & 29 & 40 & 500 \\ 80 & 10 & 19 & 200 \end{pmatrix}$

c) Weight matrix: $W = \begin{pmatrix} 10 & 50 & 14 & 40 \\ 60 & 30 & 40 & 70 \\ 50 & 40 & 70 & 15 \\ 30 & 35 & 50 & 20 \\ 20 & 30 & 40 & 10 \\ 25 & 40 & 30 & 60 \\ 45 & 35 & 7 & 10 \end{pmatrix}$

2) *Mathematical model:*

$$Max \ Z(x) = 10x_{11} + 40x_{12} + 5x_{13} + 100x_{14}$$
$$60x_{21} + 10x_{22} + 200x_{23} + 50x_{24}$$
$$30x_{31} + 150x_{32} + 90x_{33} + 15x_{34}$$
$$2x_{41} + 48x_{42} + 120x_{43} + 80x_{44}$$
$$15x_{51} + 30x_{52} + 60x_{53} + 100x_{54}$$
$$5x_{61} + 29x_{62} + 40x_{63} + 500x_{64}$$
$$80x_{71} + 10x_{72} + 19x_{73} + 200x_{74}$$

S.t.

$$10x_{11} + 60x_{12} + 50x_{13} + 30x_{14} + 20x_{15} + 25x_{16} + 45x_{17} \leq 100$$
$$50x_{21} + 30x_{22} + 40x_{23} + 35x_{24} + 30x_{25} + 40x_{26} + 35x_{27} \leq 150$$
$$14x_{31} + 40x_{32} + 70x_{33} + 50x_{34} + 40x_{35} + 30x_{36} + 7x_{37} \leq 70$$
$$40x_{41} + 70x_{42} + 15x_{43} + 20x_{44} + 10x_{45} + 60x_{46} + 10x_{47} \leq 90$$
$$x_{11} + x_{21} + x_{31} + x_{41} + x_{51} + x_{61} + x_{71} = 1$$
$$x_{12} + x_{22} + x_{32} + x_{42} + x_{52} + x_{62} + x_{72} = 1$$
$$x_{13} + x_{23} + x_{33} + x_{43} + x_{53} + x_{63} + x_{73} = 1$$
$$x_{14} + x_{24} + x_{34} + x_{44} + x_{54} + x_{64} + x_{74} = 1$$
$$x_{15} + x_{25} + x_{35} + x_{45} + x_{55} + x_{65} + x_{75} = 1$$
$$x_{16} + x_{26} + x_{36} + x_{46} + x_{56} + x_{66} + x_{76} = 1$$
$$x_{17} + x_{27} + x_{37} + x_{47} + x_{575} + x_{76} + x_{77} = 1$$
$$x_{ij} \in \{0, 1\}, \ i = 1, \ldots, 7 \ j = 1, \ldots, 7$$

[4.4]

4.6. The generalized multiassignment problem

The generalized multiassignment problem (GMAP) is a generalization of AP in which case agents can be assigned to different jobs. Numerous real-world applications can be modeled as a GMAP as it is the case of a distributed database system where each file is stored in multiple sites for more reliable and faster response time. This AP variant yields to the following mathematical formulation:

$$Min \ Z(x) = \sum_{i=1}^{m} \sum_{j=1}^{n} c_{ij} x_{ij}$$

S.t.

$$\sum_{j=1}^{n} x_{ij} \leq t_i i = 1 \ldots, n$$
$$\sum_{i=1}^{n} x_{ij} 1j = 1, \ldots, n$$
$$x_{ij} \in \{1, 0\} \ \forall i, j$$

[4.5]

where t_j is a parameter such that $t_i \leq n$ for $j = 1, .., n$. If $t_j = 1$, the GMAP is reduced to the basic AP.

4.6.1. *An example*

For illustration, we address a GMAP with $n = 7$ agents and $n = 7$ jobs. We also assume that:

1) *Input data:*

a) Number of agents = number of jobs = $n = 7$.

b) The cost matrix $C_{(7 \times 7)}$ is written as follows:

$$C = \begin{pmatrix} 10 & 20 & 100 & 3 & 70 & 90 & 25 \\ 60 & 50 & 40 & 10 & 200 & 300 & 30 \\ 150 & 200 & 30 & 70 & 500 & 100 & 50 \\ 10 & 12 & 400 & 30 & 90 & 100 & 230 \\ 19 & 30 & 40 & 300 & 120 & 40 & 50 \\ 45 & 25 & 70 & 100 & 150 & 11 & 400 \\ 500 & 20 & 30 & 50 & 300 & 130 & 350 \end{pmatrix}$$

c) The number of assignments t_i, for each agent i ($i = 1, \ldots, 7$) are reported in what follows:

Parameter	t_1	t_2	t_2	t_2	t_2	t_2	t_2
Value	2	3	1	1	2	4	1

2) *Mathematical formulation:*

$$\begin{aligned} Max\ Z(x) = &10x_{11} + 20x_{12} + 100x_{13} + 3x_{14} + 70x_{15} + 90x_{16} + 25x_{17} \\ &60x_{21} + 50x_{22} + 40x_{23} + 10x_{24} + 200x_{25} + 300x_{26} + 30x_{27} \\ &150x_{31} + 200x_{32} + 30x_{33} + 70x_{34} + 500x_{35} + 100x_{36} + 50x_{37} \\ &10x_{41} + 12x_{42} + 400x_{43} + 30x_{44} + 90x_{45} + 100x_{46} + 230x_{47} \\ &19x_{51} + 30x_{52} + 40x_{53} + 300x_{54} + 120x_{55} + 40x_{56} + 50x_{57} \\ &45x_{61} + 25x_{62} + 70x_{63} + 100x_{64} + 150x_{65} + 11x_{66} + 400x_{67} \\ &500x_{71} + 20x_{72} + 30x_{73} + 50x_{74} + 300x_{75} + 130x_{76} + 350x_{77} \end{aligned}$$

$S.t.$

$$x_{11} + x_{12} + x_{13} + x_{14} + x_{15} + x_{16} + x_{17} \leq 2$$
$$x_{21} + x_{22} + x_{23} + x_{24} + x_{25} + x_{26} + x_{27} \leq 3$$
$$x_{31} + x_{32} + x_{33} + x_{34} + x_{35} + x_{36} + x_{37} \leq 1$$
$$x_{41} + x_{42} + x_{43} + x_{44} + x_{45} + x_{46} + x_{47} \leq 1$$
$$x_{51} + x_{52} + x_{53} + x_{54} + x_{55} + x_{56} + x_{57} \leq 2$$
$$x_{61} + x_{62} + x_{63} + x_{64} + x_{65} + x_{66} + x_{67} \leq 4$$
$$x_{71} + x_{72} + x_{73} + x_{74} + x_{75} + x_{76} + x_{77} \leq 1$$
$$x_{11} + x_{21} + x_{31} + x_{41} + x_{51} + x_{61} + x_{71} = 1$$
$$x_{12} + x_{22} + x_{32} + x_{42} + x_{52} + x_{62} + x_{72} = 1$$
$$x_{13} + x_{23} + x_{33} + x_{43} + x_{53} + x_{63} + x_{73} = 1$$
$$x_{14} + x_{24} + x_{34} + x_{44} + x_{54} + x_{64} + x_{74} = 1$$
$$x_{15} + x_{25} + x_{35} + x_{45} + x_{55} + x_{65} + x_{75} = 1$$
$$x_{16} + x_{26} + x_{36} + x_{46} + x_{56} + x_{66} + x_{76} = 1$$
$$x_{17} + x_{27} + x_{37} + x_{47} + x_{575} + x_{76} + x_{77} = 1$$
$$x_{ij} \in \{0,1\}, \quad i = 1,\ldots,7 \quad j = 1,\ldots,7$$

[4.6]

4.7. Weighted assignment problem

The basic AP can be extended to handle weights for the assignment of agents to jobs. It consists of an alternative formulation of the basic AP as a special case of the weighted assignment problem (WAP) as it can be seen as the simplest case where weights are assumed to be 1 for all assignment configurations. We define a binary variable X_{ijk} as follows:

$$X_{ijk} = \begin{array}{l} 1, \text{ if task } j \text{ is completed by agent } i \text{ at performance level } k \\ 0, \text{ otherwise} \end{array}$$

The WAP formulation is:

$$Min \; \sum_{i=1}^{m} \sum_{j=1}^{n} \sum_{k \in k_{ij}} c_{ijk} x_{ijk}$$

$S.t.$

$$\sum_{i=1}^{m} \sum_{k \in k_{ij}} x_{ijk} = 1 \, j = 1,..,n$$
$$a_i \leq \sum_{j=1}^{n} \sum_{k \in K_{ij}} r_{ijk} X_{ijk} \leq b_i \, i = 1,..,m$$
$$\sum_{i=1}^{m} \sum_{k \in K_{ij}} S_{ijk} X_{ijk}$$
$$ijk = \{1,0\} \quad \forall i,j,k$$

[4.7]

– The objective function of model [4.7] minimizes the total assignment cost that covers both agents, jobs and performance levels.

– The first set of constraints of the formulation [4.7] ensure that each job j is performed by agent i at a certain performance level k. And a performance level k_{ij} is fixed for each agent i and tasks j.

– The second set of constraints of model [4.7] refers to the resource consumption limits of each job. It is clear that when there is no boundary on the used resource ($a_i = 0$), the WAP becomes a GAP.

4.8. Generalized quadratic assignment problem

The generalized quadratic assignment problem (GQAP) deals with the assignment of a set of facilities $j = 1, \ldots, n$ to a set of sites $i = 1, .., m$, while the assignment cost and traffic cost are minimized and do not exceed the capacity of the total weight of all facilities assigned. The objective function of the GAP is replaced by:

$$Min \sum_{i=1}^{m} \sum_{j=1}^{n} c_{ij} x_{ij} + \gamma \sum_{i=1}^{m} \sum_{j=1}^{n} \sum_{o=1}^{m} \sum_{p=1}^{n} \alpha_{i_o} \beta_{j_p} x_{ij} x_{op} \qquad [4.8]$$

where α_{i_o} is the distance between sites i and o, β_{j_p} is the traffic intensity between facilities p and j and γ is the unit traffic cost.

The mathematical model of the GQAP is written as follows:

$$Min \; \sum_{i=1}^{m} \sum_{j=1}^{n} c_{ij} x_{ij} + \gamma \sum_{i=1}^{m} \sum_{j=1}^{n} \sum_{o=1}^{m} \sum_{p=1}^{n} \alpha_{i_o} \beta_{j_p} x_{ij} x_{op}$$
$$S.t.$$
$$\sum_{i=1}^{n} w_{ij} x_{ij} \leq W_j \qquad\qquad j = 1, \ldots, m \qquad\qquad [4.9]$$
$$\sum_{j=1}^{m} x_{ij} = 1 \qquad\qquad\quad i = 1, \ldots, n$$

Authors have proposed a linearization for the GQAP based on the quadratic assignment problem linearization by Frieze and Jadegar (1983). A mimetic algorithm for the GQAP was proposed by Gordeau *et al.* (2006). They also mentioned an application in the management of container yards where the problem consists of the location of container groups in the storage area so that the yard handling movements are minimized.

4.9. The bottleneck GAP

The bottleneck GAP (BGAP) is a variation of the GAP proposed by Mazzola and Neebe (1988, 1993) and Martello and Toth (1995). It tries to minimize the maximum penalty of assigning n items into m knapsacks. In this case, the objective function is replaced by the following:

$$Min(Max c_{ij} x_{ij}) \quad i = 1, .., m \ \ j = 1, .., n \qquad [4.10]$$

Applications of the BGAP, presented by Martello and Toth (1995), belong to the public sector like n urban areas have to be assigned to m schools and the objective is to minimize the maximum travel time.

4.10. The multilevel GAP

The multilevel generalized assignment problem (MGAP) is a variant of the GAP in which agents can execute tasks at different efficiency levels and with different costs. It was first described in the context of large-scale allocations of tasks to machines. It deals with the determination of the minimum cost assignment of tasks to agents with varying efficiency levels. More than the classical GAP, agents can perform tasks at more than one level.

An additional set of constraints is inserted in the basic model:

$$\sum_{j=1}^{n} \sum_{k \in k_{ij}} r_{ijk} x_{ijk} \leq b_i \, i = 1, .., m \qquad [4.11]$$

MGAP can also be considered as a special case of the WAP when $a_i = 0$.

A fuzzy genetic multiobjective optimization algorithm for the MGAP was proposed and applied on the task-operator-machine AP in the clothing industry. The main objective is to minimize the total execution time and the secondary objectives are to minimize the deviation from perfect load balance among the operators, to limit the inter-operator communication cost, the number of machines and the number of operators. In order to avoid the nonlinearity and the complexity of the secondary objectives, they were using fuzzy penalty functions then relaxed the genetic multiobjective algorithm for the solution of the relaxed problem was proposed.

A first exact algorithm for the MGAP based on branch-and-price is proposed to solve small scaled instances. It consists of a decomposition of the original problem into a master problem with set-partitioning constraints and a pricing subproblem which is a multiple-choice knapsack problem.

4.11. The elastic GAP

The elastic GAP (EGAP) was studied as a set of agents allowed to violate capacity constraints at additional cost. The objective function of the elastic GAP is as follows:

$$\text{Min} \sum_{i=1}^{m} \sum_{j=1}^{n} C_{ij} X_{ij} + \sum_{i=1}^{m} (d_i u_i + e_i v_i) \qquad [4.12]$$

where variables u_j and v_j define respectively non-negative undertime and overtime, and which state the idle resource of agent i and the additional resources used by agent i. Constraints [1.2] in the classical GAP are replaced with the following:

$$\sum_{j=1}^{n} R_{ij}X_{ij} + u_i - v_i = b_i \quad i = 1,..,m \qquad [4.13]$$

Nauss (2004) has defined upper bounds for the predefined variables as follows:

$$0 \leq u_i \leq g_i \quad i = 1,..,m$$
$$0 \leq v_i \leq h_i \quad i = 1,..,m$$

He proposed a branch and bound algorithm by using linear programming cuts, Lagrangian relaxation and penalties tests. He also performed feasible solution generators to decrease the upper bound.

4.12. The multiresource GAP

The multiresource GAP (MRGAP) is another variant of the GAP, where a number of different constraining resources are associated with each agent. In this variant, the capacity constraints [1.2] of the classical GAP are replaced by the following:

$$\sum_{j=1}^{n} r_{ijq}x_{ij} \leq b_{iq} \qquad i = 1,..,m \; q = 1,..,Q$$

where each agent i is constrained by a set of resources $q = 1,..,Q$. Then for each agent i and for each resource q, there is b_{iq} unit of resources available. For each resource q, r_{ijq} is the resource required by the task j and used by the agent i.

Various real case studies can be modeled as MRGAP, the typical one arises as a subproblem in solving the vehicle routing problem, where the others appear in distributed computer systems, job shop scheduling and telecommunication network design.

The dynamic MRGAP is also investigated where the demands for tasks and capacity assignment are dynamic. A generalization of the MRGAP, namely the collectively capacitated GAP, where different constraining resources are collectively associated with all agents rather than with each agent individually.

4.13. Solution approaches for solving the AP

4.13.1. *A greedy algorithm for the AP*

The greedy algorithm specifically designed for the AP consists of proceeding in terms of the most cost saving assignment configuration. In fact, given the cost matrix C that outputs c_{ij} costs of assigning $agent_i$ to job_j, the idea is to select the minimum cost for each line of C if the corresponding job is not already handled. Hence, the greedy algorithm proceeds as stated in the following algorithm:

Algorithm 9 A greedy algorithm for the AP

1: For each agent $i = 1, \ldots, n$, let $j_i \leftarrow min_{j \in \{1,\ldots,n\}} c_{ij}$
2: If job j is not yet handled by another agent, then assign agent i to job j
3: For $k = 1, \ldots, n$
4: If $w_k \leq W'$
   – Load item k of the ranked list
   – $W' \leftarrow W' - w_k$
5: end for

4.13.2. *A genetic algorithm for the AP*

4.13.2.1. *Solution encoding*

The simplest way to represent a chromosome for the AP is to design an array of length n in which each position i indicates the job to which agent i is assigned. To well illustrate this encoding, we consider the assignment of $n = 7$ agents to 7 jobs as reported in the following scheme:

$$\boxed{2|4|6|5|7|1|3}$$

This encoding yields to the assignment of:

AGENT	$Agent_1$	$Agent_2$	$Agent_3$	$Agent_4$	$Agent_5$	$Agent_6$	$Agent_7$
JOB	Job_2	Job_4	Job_6	Job_5	Job_7	Job_1	Job_3

4.13.2.2. *Crossover*

One way to simply design the crossover for the AP is to randomly select two chromosomes from the currently processing population. The crossover that truncates two given chromosomes reconstitutes two new ones by the concatenation of different fragments. The two chromosomes obtained are readjusted in the sense that each agent is assigned to a different job, then evaluated in terms of their fitnesses. For example, if we consider the following two solutions:

$$\boxed{2|4|6|5\|7|1|3}$$

$$\boxed{5|3|1|6\|2|4|7}$$

The new chromosomes obtained, whenever the fourth position is the crossover point, are:

$$\boxed{2|4|6|5|2|4|7}$$

$$\boxed{5|3|1|6|7|1|3}$$

4.13.2.3. *Mutation*

Randomly applied to explore other areas in the solution space, the mutation operator in the GA applied to the AP uses a probability which is known to be inversely proportional to the population size N. Thus, after applying the crossover, an individual can be selected from the current population for mutation. The proposed method operates by randomly selecting a solution x from the currently inspected population for an eventual improvement.

| 2 | 4 | 6 | 5 | 7 | 1 | 3 |

Algorithm 10 A genetic algorithm for the AP

1: Initialization:

– Generate randomly an initial population P_0 of N chromosomes

– Evaluate each chromosome by calculating its fitness function

2: Iterative process:

1) Select two chromosomes x and y according to their fitness functions or randomly

2) Apply the crossover or mutation depending on the iteration number

- *Crossover:* generate two offsprings $\{z_1, z_2\} \leftarrow one-point-crossover(x,y)$

- *Mutation:* obtain two offsprings $\{z_1, z_2\} \leftarrow mutation(x,y)$

3) Evaluate the obtained offspring z_1 and z_2 by their fitness functions

4) Memorize the best encountered solution z

5) Check the stopping criterion

4.14. Conclusion

Many real-life applications are to be modeled as an AP, as production planning, supply chain, telecommunication and facility layout.

In this chapter, we presented some variants, applications and solution procedures of the AP. Each problem variant is detailed and mathematically stated. Some illustrations were provided to show the problem complexity and difficulty of a mathematical formulation whenever the problem becomes large. As in the previous chapters, greedy and GA approaches are adapted for the AP.

5

The Resource Constrained Project Scheduling Problem

5.1. Introduction

The resource-constrained project scheduling problem (RCPSP) is a widely studied optimization problem in the literature of operations research, especially in scheduling theory. Known to be able to model a large panoply of practical applications, such as manpower scheduling [DEN 11], grid computing [LO 08], classroom arrangement [DAM 06] and surveillance problems [DRI 14], it outputs the cost saving sequence of tasks to be scheduled while fulfilling specific structural constraints. Basically, the RCPSP consists of planning a set of tasks to be accomplished by several resources. Each task necessitates one or numerous resources that constitute a mode.

The RCPSP is a. It is widely known to be notoriously difficult to solve due to the employment of scarce resources as well as precedence relations between activities. Considering these constraints, the problem consists of finding an efficient arrangement of activities that leads to a minimal completion time of the project.

Besides the problem's relevance with respect to the applicability in real-world situations, the RCPSP has attracted a considerable attention from both researchers and practitioners. Blazewicz *et al.* have proved that the RCPSP belongs to the class of the strongly non-deterministic polynomial-time ($\mathcal{NP}$)-hard problems. Therefore, a very large body of literature is devoted to solve it, given place to various exact and approximation methods on the wide variety of variants and assumptions. Exact methods involve the use of enumerative schemes and often used to solve small-sized problems at optimality. However, these algorithms are far from being efficient in terms of computational time when solving large-scale problems. Approximation methods and, more specifically, metaheuristic algorithms appear to be robust in finding good solutions in a reasonable computational time. The related approximation approaches include the genetic algorithm, the particle swarm optimization, the simulated annealing, the tabu search, the ant colony optimization and hybrid algorithms. We refer the readers to [KOL 06] for a comprehensive review on RCPSPs. This chapter is structured as follows. In the first part, we will define the basic version of the RCPSP. Then, we will focus on the RCPSP variants. One important issue is the outline of the adaptation of the greedy and genetic algorithm (GA) for the RCPSP.

5.2. Graph modeling of the RCPSP

The RCPSP can be modeled as an acyclic graph $G = (V, E)$ where:

– V denotes the set of tasks: $|V| = n$.

– E designates precedence requirements between tasks.

If a node $x \in V$ is not connected to any other node of V, its corresponding tasks is called a floating task that can be accomplished without any precedence constraint. In such a case, G is not connected. Graphically, the RCPSP is reported as follows:

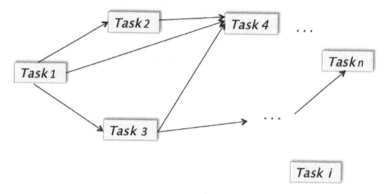

Figure 5.1. *Graph representation of the RCPSP*

5.3. Notation

The following main symbols are used to model the RCPSP:

Symbols	Explanation
i	Task index, $i \in \{1, \dots, n\}$
k	Resource index, $k \in \{1, \dots, |R|\}$
P_i	Set of immediate predecessors of task i
E_k	Constant amount of renewable resource k is available at any time
$[a_i, b_i]$	Time window on the completion of task i
T	An upper bound on the makespan
d_i	processing time of activity i
F_i	Finishing time of task i
y_i^t	Equal to 1 if task i starts at the beginning of period $t \in T$ and 0 otherwise
x_{ik}	1 if task i is accomplished by resource k and 0 otherwise

5.4. Single-mode RCPSP

Single-mode resource-constrained project scheduling problem (SM-RCPSP) can be defined as a set of resources with limited capacities to accomplish a set of tasks during a time interval. Each task is accomplished using one or several resources, called mode. Tasks are interrelated by precedence constraints that enforce the starting time of one task only if all its predecessors were accomplished.

The SM-RCPSP is as an acyclic graph where nodes represent tasks and edges represent model precedence relations. Based on such assumptions, the objective of the RCPSP problem is to find the most cost-saving assignment of the resources to time period while fulfilling resource capacity limits. The resources can be renewable from period to period or non-renewable, in which case once a resource is completely consumed, it cannot be reutilized in later stages.

The RCPSP can be stated as follows. A project with n activities labeled $i = 1, \ldots, n$ has to be planned without preemption. Due to technological requirements, precedence relations need to be pointed out. These relationships are given by sets of immediate predecessors P_i, indicating that an activity i may not be started before each of its predecessors $j \in P_i$ is completed. Precedence relations can be represented by an activity-on-node network which is assumed to be acyclic. There are $|R|$ renewable resource types with r_{ik} denoting the resource requirements of activity i with respect to resource k.

The objective of the problem is to schedule each activity of a project subject to precedence and resource constraints, in order to minimize the project makespan. Numerous objectives can be optimized in the modeling of the RCPSP as follows:

– *The minimum makespan*: this is the most adopted objective in the literature. It corresponds to the minimization of the total time period required for accomplishing the whole set of tasks.

– *The cost minimization*: this consists of the reduction of the total cost of involved resources.

– *The quality maximization*: this corresponds to the improvement of the quality of the project.

5.4.1. *Mathematical modeling of the SM-RCPSP*

Based on the above definitions, the problem can be represented formally as the following time-indexed formulation:

$$Min \ Z(x) = Max_{i=1}^n \ F_i$$
$$S.t.$$

$$\sum_{i=1}^n r_{ik} \, x_{ik} \leq E_k, \ \forall k = 1,\ldots,|R|$$
$$\sum_{t=0}^T y_i^t \leq 1, \ i = 1,\ldots,n \qquad [5.1]$$
$$\sum_{t \in T} t \, (y_i^t - y_j^t) \geq F_j, \ \forall j \in P_i$$
$$F_i \geq \sum_{t \in T} t y_i^t + d_i, \ i = 1,\ldots,n$$
$$x_{ik}, y_i^t \in \{0,1\}, \ \forall i = 1,\ldots,n, \ \forall t \in T, a_i \leq F_i \leq b_i$$

– The objective function of model (5.1) symbolizes the project makespan to be minimized while fulfilling problem constraints.

– The first set of constraints takes care of the limited quantity of the renewable resource constraints.

– The second set of constraints imposes that each task is started at most at one time over the planning horizon T.

– The third set of constraints ensures that the starting time of task i that follows task j is greater than or equal to the completion of task j, F_j.

– The fourth set of constraints establishes the fact that the completion time of task i is greater than or equal to the sum of starting times and processing times.

– The fifth set of constraints states logical binary restrictions on decision variables.

5.4.2. *An example of an SM-RCPSP*

Let us consider an RCPSP with $n = 4$ tasks and only one renewable resource available with 4 units in each period. Figure 5.2 shows the optimal schedule with $Z(x) = 8$, where both the precedence constraint and resource constraint are satisfied. Problem data are reported in Table 5.1.

Activity i	P_i	d_i	r_1
1	-	3	1
2	1	4	2
3	1	2	2
4	2, 3	1	3

Table 5.1. *An RCPSP with* $n = 4$ *and* $|R| = 1$

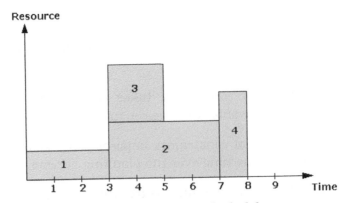

Figure 5.2. *The optimal schedule*

For the SM-RCPSP, each task has a single execution mode: both the activity duration and its requirements for a set of resources are assumed to be fixed in advance, and only one execution mode is available for any task. The set of tasks is constrained by the precedence relationships, e.g. task i must be completed before starting the task j. Broadly, there are two precedence conditions: cases in which activity j can start at any time following the completion of activity i, or cases in which activity j must start within some time window following the completion of activity.

5.5. Multimode RCPSP

The multimode RCPSP ($MM - RCPSP$) is defined as an RCPSP where each task has to be processed in one of several modes. Each mode implies a different option in terms of cost, processing time and amount of a particular resource for achieving a task.

For example, a single worker who might finish a job in 10 h is mode 1, whereas two workers who might finish the job in 5 h are mode 2. The resources available for completing the tasks can be classified as either renewable or non-renewable. Non-renewable resources are depleted after a certain amount of consumption, while renewable resources have the same amount of availability in every period.

5.6. RCPSP with time windows

The RCPSPTW extends the optimization model. The RCPSPTW is a specific formulation of the basic problem underlying a number of scheduling applications and is considered to be particularly difficult due to the presence of temporal separation constraints (in particular, maximum time lags) between project activities. In fact, finding a feasible schedule alone is NP-hard. The classical RCPSP tries to find a suitable solution in order to optimize the makespan, i.e. to find the best resource allocation for a given set of activities.

But, in reality, the problem of scheduling demands the consideration of several objectives, generally the conflict, as the length of time, weather of the project and the cost of the resources were used to execute the activities of the project.

We are interested in the problem of project organization in limited means (RCPSP), this is one of the most known problems of cumulative organization. So the RCPSP with time windows (RCPSPTW).

The RCPSP with time windows has been widely studied in operations research (OR) literature (see [BRU 12] for a survey).

This scheduling problem derives from a project management environment in which the activities represent the stages that must be executed to realize the completion of the project and are subjected to the partial constraints of order which reflect dependencies in the progress of the project and so are dependent on the constraints of the time that indicates the duration of the beginning of such activities. The RCPSP version with time windows (RCPSP/max) is an extended formulation of the basic problem which underlies a number of scheduling applications and is considered particularly difficult due to the presence of temporal separation constraints (in particular, maximum time lags) between project activities.

5.7. Solution approaches for solving the RCPSP

5.7.1. *A greedy algorithm for the RCPSP*

The greedy algorithm is adapted for the RCPSP. The main incentive is to generate, in a concurrent time, good quality solutions that tend to be optimal mainly for small-sized RCPSPs.

Algorithm 11 A greedy algorithm for the RCPSP

1: For each task $i = 1, \ldots, n$ to be scheduled during the period $t \in T$

Check the availability and resource feasibility of the mode for accomplishing task i

2: If the mode is available, then check the precedence requirements

Else delay the accomplishment of task i for the next period

3: If i is a floating task, then check only resource requirements.

5.7.2. A genetic algorithm for the RCPSP

Numerous versions of the GA for solving the RCPSP were developed in the existing literature that differ in terms of the algorithm's features such as:

– solution encoding;

– feasibility or unfeasibility of the solutions;

– generation of the initial population;

– crossover: one-point or two-point crossing of the chromosomes trying to improve the solution quality;

– mutation: the exchange of two tasks or the moving of one task from one period to another;

– stopping criterion, which will be the maximum number of iterations, the running time or the number of iterations without improvement.

In the following we propose a GA for solving the SM-RCPSP in which case there is no need to mention the mode to be adopted for accomplishing tasks. As it is proven that GA provides promising solutions scheduling problems, we propose an outline of a generic version that can be adapted for other versions of the RCPSP. The general idea of the GA consists of first generating an initial population that can be a mixture of specifically designed heuristics and randomly generated solutions. Such solutions are adjusted if unfeasibility is depicted in the evaluation phase. As two classes of constraints are observed in the modeling of the RCPSP, namely task and resource constraints, the unfeasibility can be related to precedence requirements or resources capacity limits. In fact, solutions generated with standard genetic operators may tend to create infeasible individuals during the search because of the discrete and often constrained search space. During the iterative process, for each currently handled population, genetic operators are applied as the crossing of chromosomes and the exchange of solutions' fragments to obtain new offspring. The set of solutions obtained is readjusted to become feasible. For a diversity purpose, the mutation tries to guide the search space to other areas. Hence, a task is switched to be assigned to a different time period if precedence and resource constraints are fulfilled. It can be noted that premature convergence may lead to search stagnation on restricted regions of the search space instead of convergence toward an unexplored area. In this respect, considering the exploration ability of GAs, we can choose a termination criterion that varies in terms of the problem size, or a combination of termination criteria. This process iterates until reaching the stopping rule.

5.7.2.1. *Chromosome encoding*

The encoding of the chromosomes is designed as an n-sized vector that reports the periods in which each task is scheduled.

Task	1	2	3	4	...	n
Period	5	4	3	5	...	3

Each generated chromosome should be checked for feasibility.

5.7.2.2. *Selection*

In nature, the selection of individuals is achieved by survival of the fittest. The more one individual is adapted to the environment, the bigger its chances to survive, create offspring and thus transfer its genes to the next generation.

In evolutionary algorithms, the selection of the best individuals is based on an evaluation of a fitness function or fitness functions. Examples of such fitness function are the sum of the square error between the wanted system response and the real one; the distance of the poles of the closed-loop system to the desired poles, etc. If the optimization problem is a minimization one, then individuals with small value of the fitness function will have bigger chances for recombination and, respectively, for generating offspring:

– evaluate fitness of each solution in current population (e.g. ability to classify/discriminate);

– selection of individuals for survival based on probabilistic function of fitness;

– on average, mean fitness of individuals increases;

– may include elitist step to ensure the survival of fittest individual.

5.7.2.3. *Crossover*

The incentive behind using the crossover operator for improving currently processed solutions is to combine pairs of selected chromosomes that are the "best" according to the selection criterion, in the hope of improving the fitness of obtained solutions. The crossover occurs according to a prefixed crossover probability. The main steps of the crossover are:

– the selection of two chromosomes, using the elitist method or at random;

– the selection of crossover points is generally random;

– individuals not crossed are carried over in population.

Two types of crossover are pointed out: one-point and two-point crossover.

1) *One-point crossover:* two individuals, called $parent_1$ and $parent_2$, are selected. Then an integer number q is generated randomly between 1 and J to obtain two new individuals: Son 11....q and Son 2q....j. Activities in positions i = 1...q in Son 1 are taken from parent 1. Activities in positions i = q + 1; ...; J in Son 1 are taken from Parent 2. As an example, let us consider Parent 1 1,3,2,5,4,6 and Parent 2 2,4,6,1,3,5. With q = 3, Son 1 1,3,2,6,4,5.

2) *Two-point crossover:* two-point crossover is an extension of one-point crossover. Two integer numbers q1 and q2 are randomly generated with 1 ? q1 ? q2 ? j. Now, Son 1 is generated with activities list on positions i = 1.....q1 taken from Parent 1, activities in positions i = q1 + 1; ...; q2 are taken from Parent 2 and finally positions i = q2 + 1, ..., j are again taken from Parent 1. By taking the same example of the previous section, let us consider Parent 1 1,3,2,5,4,6 and Parent 2 2,4,6,1,3,5. With q1 = 1 and q2 = 2, Son 1 is 1,2,4,3,5,6.

5.7.2.4. *Mutation*

The mutation is a random operation that consists of substituting one gene with another one within a chromosome in order to diversify the solutions and produce new points in the solution space. We proceed by changing one or more elements of the chromosome.

4	1	3	8	0	7	3	1	3	5	1
4	1	3	8	0	7	3	8	3	5	1

Table 5.2. *Chromosome mutation*

GA consists of encoding a solution to a string called chromosome. Each chromosome is composed of a set of elements called genes. Then, GA apply recombination operators to these solutions through crossover and mutation operators to produce offspring chromosomes. Thus, three natural operators are used for the exploitation of the solution space:

– *Reproduction operators*: this consists of copying pairs of individual strings according to their fitness values. In the reproduction process, we select the best individuals with higher fitness values in order to contribute in the next generation.

– *Crossover operation*: in order to maintain diversification and to generate differential individuals, crossover operator creates an offspring that contains a combination of genes from its parents. Thus, the crossover process consists of combining the best features of each chromosome by exchanging the genetic material between two individuals.

– *Mutation operators*: this operator is used to diversify the solutions and to avoid stagnation around local optima. The mutation process consists of changing the position by modifying a 1 to a 0 and vice versa. Thus, this process contributes to the production of new points in the solution space.

The parameter used in the GA is population size, number of generations, crossover rate and mutation rate.

Algorithm 12 A genetic algorithm for the RCPSP

1: INPUT P_0: The initial population of size S
   $cross_p$: The crossover probability
   C_i: The offspring population at generation i
   P_i: The parent population at generation i
2: OUTPUT P_{i+1}: The updated parent population at generation
   $i + 1$
   C_i: The updated offspring population at generation $i + 1$
3: INITIALIZATION Randomly generate P_0
   Fitness evaluation of P_0
   $i \leftarrow 1$
   $P_i \leftarrow P_0$
4: LOOPING PROCEDURE **DO**
   Apply the crossover operator according to $cross_p$:
      Generate the offspring population C_i
      Generate a neighbor $N(s) = LS(s, t, t')$
      If $Z(N(s)) < Z(s)$ then $s \leftarrow N(s)$
   $R_i \leftarrow$ non-domination sort $(C_i \cup P_i)$
   $i \leftarrow i + 1$
   WHILE *stopping criteria not met*

5.8. Conclusion

This chapter has presented the RCPSP that constitutes a hard constrained optimization problem, naturally designed as a graph in which nodes designate the set of tasks to be scheduled and the edges express precedence constraints. As this problem can model a large variety of real-world applications, we stated its mathematical formulation and some illustrative examples to show the difficulty of reaching an optimal solution even for small-scaled instances. We have also given an overview of some of its variants that include the number of modes to be used for accomplishing tasks and time window constraints. As solution approaches for solving the RCPSP, we have exposed an adaptation of the greedy algorithm and a detalied version of the GA.

6

Spanning Tree Problems

6.1. Introduction

One of the most important concepts of graph theory is that of a tree. Tree optimization problems arise in a surprisingly large number of applications such as telecommunications, facility location, computer networking, energy distribution and manufacturing. In addition, the concept of the tree is a mathematical entity that poses significant modeling and algorithmic challenges to illustrate many key ideas from the field of combinatorial optimization. Many real-life combinatorial optimization problems belong to this class of problems and consequently there is a large and growing interest in both theoretical and practical aspects. For some of these problems there are polynomial-time algorithms, while most of them are *NP*-hard. Mainly, it means that it is not possible to guarantee that an exact solution to the problem can be found and we have to settle for heuristics and approximate solution approaches with performance guarantees. In this chapter, we consider four variants of spanning tree problems: the minimum spanning tree (MST) problem, the generalized minimum spanning tree (GMST) problem, the k-cardinality problem and the capacitated minimum spanning tree (CMST) problem. For each variant, we present its definition, mathematical formulation and two different resolution approaches. The first approach is greedy and the second approach is based on genetic algorithm (GA).

6.2. Minimum spanning tree problem

Trees are the minimal graphs that connect any set of nodes, thereby permitting all the nodes to communicate with each other without any extra arcs to ensure connectivity. Therefore, if the edges have positive costs, the minimum cost subgraph connecting all the nodes is a tree that spans all of the nodes with a minimum cost. The MST problem consists of finding a tree that contains all the nodes of a graph and that minimizes the overall weight of the edges in the tree.

6.2.1. Notation

Following are the main symbols used to model the MST problem:

Symbols	Explanation
G	A directed weighted graph
V	Set of nodes $\{1, \ldots, n\}$
E	Set of edges $\{1, \ldots, m\}$
n	Number of nodes
m	Number of edges
W	Function cost associated to each edge e in E
w_e	The cost of edge e
S	A non empty subset of nodes in V
x_e	Equals to 1 if edge e is in the spanning tree and 0 otherwise

6.2.2. Mathematical formulation

Consider the graph $G = (V, E)$. Of the many spanning trees of G that may be possible, we want to find the tree for which the sum of the costs of its links is a minimum. The integer programming formulation of the MST problem is stated as:

$$
Min \ C(x) = \sum_{e \in E} w_e x_e
$$

$$
S.t \quad \sum_{e \in E} x_e = n - 1
$$

$$
\sum_{e \in E(S)} x_e \leq |S - 1| \ \forall S \subset V \qquad \text{[6.1]}
$$

$$
x_e = 0 \text{ or } 1; \qquad \text{for all edges } e
$$

The above description corresponds to the *0-1 variable* x_e which indicates whether we select edge e as part of the chosen spanning tree. The first constraint is a cardinality constraint implying that we choose exactly $n - 1$ edges. The second constraint is the "packing" constraint which implies that the set of chosen edges contains no cycles.

6.2.3. *Algorithms for the MST problem*

The resolution of the MST tree of a graph is one of the few problems in graph theory which can be considered completely solved.

6.2.3.1. *The Kruskal algorithm*

This algorithm chooses to add into the partially formed tree the absolute shortest link which is feasible. However, the situation may arise in this algorithm in which the next shortest edge chosen from the list L may be between two nodes of the same subtree which would then make this link infeasible since its addition would close a circuit. Thus, links must be tested for feasibility before they are added to T.

Algorithm 13 The Kruskal algorithm

1: $T \leftarrow \emptyset$
2: Order the set of edges E in ascending order of cost in a list L.
3: Starting from the top of L add links to T that this addition does not close a circuit in T.
4: Repeat step 2 until $(n-1)$ links have been added. T is then the Minimum Spanning Tree of graph G.

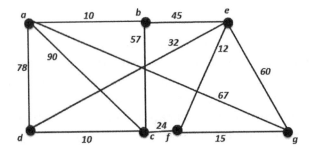

Figure 6.1. *An example of a connected valued graph with* $n = 6$

We consider the example of Chapter 2 to illustrate the Kruskal and Prim algorithms, respectively. In the Kruskal algorithm, we first start by ordering edge weights in increasing order (see Figure 6.2(a)) then we follow the algorithm in six iterations as detailed in Figure 6.2(b).

6.2.3.2. *The Prim algorithm*

We use the same example of the graph (see Figure 6.1) to illustrate the Prim algorithm. Figure 6.3 shows the steps of Prim algorithm.

Several variants of the MST problems were studied in the literature. We dedicate the following section to examine variants of this basic problem.

Edges	Weight
$d - c$	10
$a - b$	10
$e - f$	12
$f - g$	15
$c - f$	24
$e - d$	32
$b - e$	45
$b - c$	57
$e - g$	60
$a - g$	67
$a - d$	78
$a - c$	90

a)

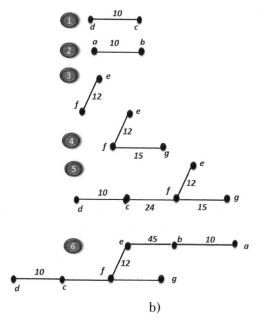

b)

Figure 6.2. *An illustrative example of the Kruskal algorithm*

Algorithm 14 The Prim algorithm

1: Let $T_s = \{v_s\}$, where v_s is any arbitrarily chosen vertex, and $A_s = \emptyset$.

2: For all $v_j \notin T_s$ find a vertex $\alpha_j \in T_s$ so that:

- $c(\alpha_j, v_j) = min_{v_i \in T_s}[c(v_i, v_j)] = \beta_j$
- and set the label of v_j as $[\alpha_j, \beta_j]$
- If no such vertex v_j can be found then set the label of v_j as $(0, \infty)$.

3: Choose that vertex v_j* so that $\beta_j* = min_{v_j \notin T_s}[\beta_j]$.

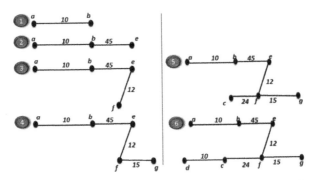

Figure 6.3. *An illustrative example of the Prim algorithm*

6.3. Generalized minimum spanning tree problem

This problem was first introduced by Myung *et al.* in 1995 [MYU]. The authors studied the particular case of the problem where we want to find a MST with exactly one node per subset. We denote that problem as EGMST. Figure 6.4 gives an example of two feasible solutions of GMST and EGMST.

The GMST has a great variety of real-world applications in many areas including the interconnection of several local networks to yield a single large network. In this case, we should select at least one node from each local network and then construct a GMST. Contrary to the MST problem, the GMST and EGMST problems are *NP*-hard.

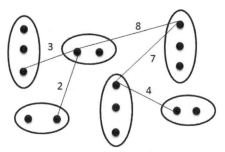

Feasible solution of EGMST Problem

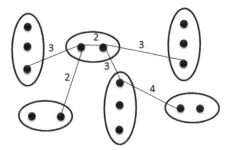

Feasible solution of GMST Problem

Figure 6.4. *An example of GMST and EGMST feasible solutions*

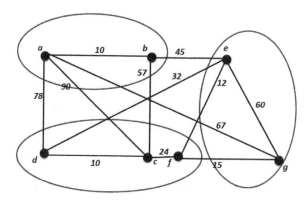

Figure 6.5. *An illustrative example of the GMST problem*

6.3.1. *Notation*

Following are the main symbols used to model the GMST problem:

Symbols	Explanation
G	A connected undirected weighted graph
V	Set of nodes $\{1, \ldots, n\}$
E	Set of edges $\{1, \ldots, m\}$
n	Number of nodes
m	Number of edges
K	Number of disjoint subsets
W	Function cost associated to each edge e in E
w_e	The cost of edge e

Given a general connected undirected graph $G = (V, E)$. The node set V is a union of K disjoint subsets $V = \bigcup_{k=1,K} V_k$ where $V_i \cap V_j = \emptyset$ for $i \neq j$. A GMST is an MST tree such that every set V_k is covered by at least one node.

6.3.2. *Mathematical formulation*

There are many mathematical formulations of the GMST problem. We present in this section a mathematical formulation based on the minimum cost multiterminal network flow problem and developed by Dror *et al.* [DOR 00a]. Let us consider a new directed valued graph $G = (V, E, C, s, t)$ such that:

$-$ V is the set of n vertices and E the set of m edges;

$-$ C a function from E in $\aleph$; c_{ij} is the maximal capacity of the edge (i, j); we denote U the maximum of capacity;

$-$ let s and t be two particular nodes called source and destination, respectively;

$-$ we define a flow function Φ from E to $\aleph$ where Φ_{ij} is the flow on (i, j). Then, we have the following properties:

- $\forall (i,j) \in E,\, 0 \leq \Phi_{ij} \leq c_{ij}$: the flow on each edge is compatible with the capacity,

- $\forall i \neq s,t;\, \sum \Phi_{sj} = \sum \Phi_{jt}$: the flow is conserved on each node,

- $F = \sum \Phi_{sj} = \sum \Phi_{jt}$: the total debit is equal to the flow entered by s and exited by t.

Figure 6.6 illustrates the new graph based on network flow.

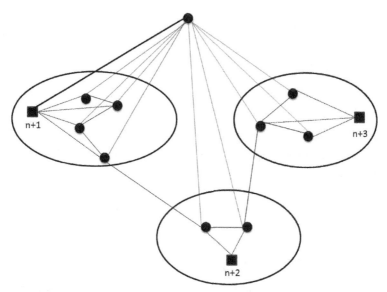

Figure 6.6. *Transformation of the graph as a network flow*

The problem now consists of finding the minimum flow F. To formulate the GMST problem as a minimum flow problem, let us consider a graph $G' = (V', E')$ from $G = (V, E)$ such that:

$- V' = V \cup \{(j, i) \in E$ such that $c_{ij} = c_{ji}.$

– Create $n + k$ dummy nodes in each subset k, where $k = 1, ..., K$. Each dummy node is linked to all nodes of each set V_k by zero cost edges $(i, n + k)$, where $i \in V_k$.

– Create a dummy node 0 as a singleton set such that $c_{oi} = M \forall i \in V$ and M is a high enough cost.

– Create K one source-one sink flow with source 0 and sinks $n + k$ with cost flow equals to 1.

– The cost on each arc $(i, j) \in U'$ is equal to a zero cost flow plus a fixed cost c_{ij}.

If we consider the partial graph $G^* = (V, F^*)$ with F^* is the set of edges carrying non-zero total flows, then it is worth noting that:

– G^* is connected;

– G^* is acyclic;

– F^* has at least one node from each subset $V_k (k = 1, ..., K)$;

– the cost of the optimal flow is equal to the sum of the costs of the edges of.

Consequently, the edges of F^* define an optimal solution for the GMST problem.

Let us now define the following decision variables:

– $x_{ij} = 1$ if arc $(i, j) \in U'$ is selected in the optimal solution, and 0 otherwise;

– $y_{ijk} = $ value of the flow $k = 1, ..., K$ on arc $(i, j) \in U'$.

The network flow formulation of the GMST problem can be stated as:

$$Min \ \sum_{(i,j) \in U'} c_{ij} x_{ij}$$

$$S.t \quad y_{ijk} - x_{ij} = 0 \qquad\qquad \forall (i,j) \in U', k = 1, ..., K$$

$$\sum_{j:(0,j) \in U'} y_{0jk} = 1 \qquad\qquad k = 1, ..., K$$

$$\sum_{j:(i,j) \in U'} y_{ijk} - \sum_{h:(h,i) \in U'} y_{hik} = 0 \ \ i = 1, ..., n, k = 1, ..., K \qquad [6.2]$$

$$\sum_{j:(j,n+k) \in U'} y_{j,n+k,k} = 1 \qquad\qquad k = 1, ..., K$$

$$x_{ij} \in \{0, 1\} \qquad\qquad \forall (i,j) \in U'$$

$$y_{ijk} eq \{0, 1\} \qquad\qquad \forall i, j, k \in V'$$

The constraint [2] shows that if the edge (i, j) is in the solution, then there exists a flow of type k between i and j. Constraints [4] and [5] are flow constraints: constraint [4] means that there is only one unit of flow of type $k(k = 2, ..., K)$ from the node $n + 1$. Constraint [5] shows that $i \in V_{n+k}$ cannot receive more than one unit of flow of type $k(k = 2, ..., K)$. Constraint [6] is the conservation's flow law. We add constraint [3] to enforce that only one arc is going from node $n + 1$.

6.3.3. Greedy approaches for the GMST problem

There are many greedy approaches to solve the GMST problem. We present here only two different greedy methods. The first method is based on the Kruskal algorithm and the second method is based on the idea of the Prim algorithm.

Algorithm 15 The greedy algorithm based on Kruskal algorithm for the GMST problem

1: Let T the spanning tree using the the Kruskal algorithm on the graph $G = (V, E)$.

2: Delete from T all redundant nodes:

    – All nodes with degree equal to 1;

    – All nodes that verify $|(V \setminus \{i\}) \cap V_k| \geq 1 \forall k = 1, ..., K$.

3: Delete from T all redundant edges:

    – Sort redundant edges (edges with redundant nodes) in decreasing order.

    – Delete edges one by one until the remaining arcs build a generalized spanning tree.

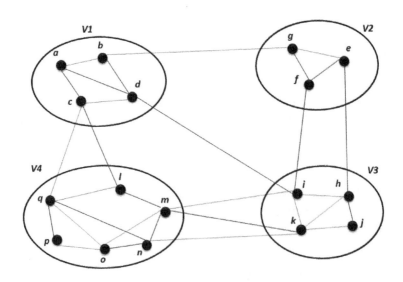

Figure 6.7. *Step 1 of the greedy algorithm based on the Kruskal algorithm*

Figure 6.7 shows step 1 of the greedy algorithm based on the Kruskal algorithm and Figure 6.8 shows step 2 in the same example.

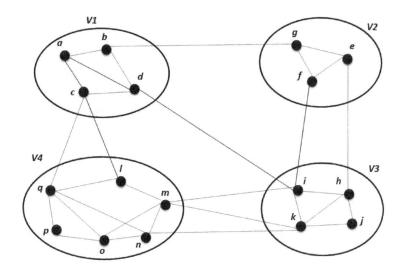

Figure 6.8. *Step 2 of the greedy algorithm based on the Kruskal algorithm*

Now, we present another greedy algorithm for the GMST problem this time based on the Prim algorithm.

Algorithm 16 The greedy algorithm based on the Prim algorithm for the GMST problem

---

1: $i = 0$.
2: **Step 1**: $i = i + 1; T_i = \emptyset; S = \{1, 2, ..., K\}$
3: **Step 2**: Find the subset V_j the nearest to V_i. Let T_i be smallest arc between V_i and V_j. $S \leftarrow S \backslash \{i, j\}$
4: **Step 3**: Find the subset $V_k (k \in S)$ the nearest to T_i. $T_i \leftarrow T_i \cup PATH(T_i, V_k), S \leftarrow S \backslash k$.
5: **Step 4**: If $S = \emptyset$ then let $c(T_i)$ the cost of T_i; otherwise go to step 3
6: **Step 5**: If $i = k$ then T_s is the solution with cost $c(T_i) = min_i c(T_i)$; otherwise go to step 1.

$PATH$ is the shortest path and needs $O(n^2)$ as its computing time. In this greedy method, we call K times the procedure $PATH$ to compute the shortest path between each subset $V_k(k = 1, ..., K)$ and the tree T_i. Consequently, this method needs $O(Kn^2)$ as its computing time. We note here that if each subset $V_k(k = 1, ..., K)$ contains one node, this algorithm is equivalent to the Prim algorithm.

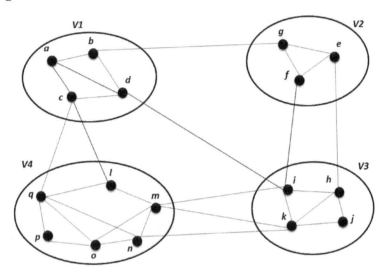

Figure 6.9. *An example of the greedy algorithm based on the Prim algorithm*

6.3.4. *Genetic algorithm for the GMST problem*

Dror *et al.* [DOR 00a] were developed a first version of a GA for the GMST problem. However, Haouari and Chaouachi [HAO 06a] developed another version of GA and this version outperforms the first one. In this section, we explain in detail this last version of GA.

6.3.4.1. *Encoding*

To represent a chromosome, we use an integer encoding for an individual with a length equal to K (number of subsets). With this encoding, we guarantee a high speed to the GA because the number of subsets K is less than the number of nodes n. Another advantage of this encoding is that all solutions are feasible; therefore, there is no need for a penalization procedure. Figure 6.10 shows an example of integer encoding of the population.

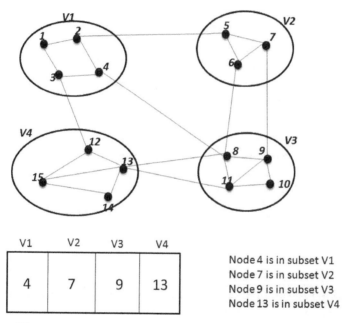

V1	V2	V3	V4
4	7	9	13

Node 4 is in subset V1
Node 7 is in subset V2
Node 9 is in subset V3
Node 13 is in subset V4

Figure 6.10. *An example of integer encoding used in the genetic algorithm for the GMST problem*

6.3.4.2. *Fitness*

To evaluate the fitness of an individual, we should solve a Steiner problem where the set of terminal nodes is T and the set of Steiner nodes is $S \backslash T$. T contains the nodes in the individual. The following figure shows the tree obtained by solving the Steiner problem with terminal nodes $4, 7, 9, 13$ and node 8 as Steiner node. The fitness of such an individual is the sum of the edges' costs. In the initial population, we randomly generate all the individuals. The size of the initial population is *popsize*.

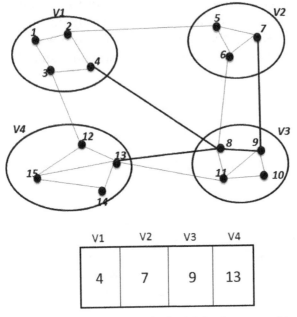

V1	V2	V3	V4
4	7	9	13

Figure 6.11. *An individual with its fitness used in the genetic algorithm for the GMST problem*

Figure 6.11 shows an example of how we obtain the fitness of an individual.

6.3.4.3. *Crossover*

We use the one-point crossover that selects two chromosomes, then exchange the two portions in order to obtain new solutions. The process can be described as follows:

4	7	3	6 ‖ 13	9	11

5	7	1	8 ‖ 14	10	12

The new chromosomes obtained, whenever the fourth position is the crossover point, are:

| 4 | 7 | 3 | 6 | 14 | 10 | 12 |

| 5 | 7 | 1 | 8 | 14 | 10 | 12 |

We note here that due to the strategy of encoding there is no need for special crossover because all obtained offsprings are feasible. The crossover operates with a probability p_c.

6.3.4.4. *Mutation*

After applying the crossover, an individual i is randomly selected from the current population with a probability p_m for mutation. The proposed method operates by randomly selecting a position p from the individual i.

| 4 | 7 | 1 | 6 | 13 | 9 | 11 |
| 4 | 7 | 2 | 6 | 13 | 9 | 11 |

We note here that the position is equal to 3 and we replace the node 1 in the subset 3 by any node from the third subset; for our case this node is 2.

6.3.4.5. *Parameters*

The table below shows the parameters used for the GA to solve the GMST problem.

Parameters	Value
Popsize	100
p_m	0.01
p_c	0.9
Number of generations	100

The proposed GA was tested on instances of Dror *et al.* [DOR 00a]. Experimental results show that the GA outperforms many other heuristics such as Ant tree and PROGRES [HAO 06a]. In fact, for all instances, it yields the best solution and in 92.5% it gives the optimal solution.

6.4. k-cardinality tree problem KCT

The edge weighted k-cardinality tree (KCT) problem is a combinatorial optimization problem introduced in 1991 by Hamacher *et al.* [HAM 91]. The KCT problem arises naturally in a variety of applications, e.g. in oil-field leasing [HAM 93], facility layout [FOU 98, FOU 92], open pit mining [PHI 97], matrix decomposition [BOR 97, BOR 98], quorum-cast routing [CHE 94] and telecommunications [GAR 97].

6.4.1. *Problem definition*

Let $G = (V, E)$ a valued graph with V being the set of nodes and E being the set of edges. The KCT problem consists of finding a tree with minimum cost having exactly k edges. The number k is less or equal to $|V| - 1$. If $k = |V| - 1$ then the problem is equivalent to the MST problem. Due to the hardness of the k-cardinality problem, in the next section we present some heuristics to solve it.

6.4.2. *An example*

Let us consider a graph with $n = 7$ and $k = 5$.

The mathematical formulation of the k-cardinality problem with $n = 7$ and $k = 5$ is written as follows:

$$Min\ C(x) = 14x_1 + 22x_2 + 10x_3 + 9x_4 + 20x_5 + 25x_6 + 14x_7 + 15x_8 + 15x_9$$

$S.t.$

$$x_1 + x_2 + x_3 + x_4 + x_5 + x_6 + x_7 + x_8 = 5$$
$$y_1 + y_2 + y_3 + y_4 + y_5 + y_6 + y_7 = 6$$
$$x_i \in \{0, 1\}, \quad i = 1, \ldots, 9$$
$$y_j \in \{0, 1\}, \quad j = 1, \ldots, 7$$

[6.3]

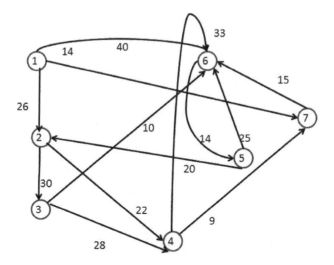

Figure 6.12. *An illustrative example of k-cardinality problem with n = 7 and k = 5*

The resolution of the KCT yields to the optimal solution, as reported in the screenshot in Figure 6.13, is $x^* = (1, 0, 1, 1, 0, 0, 1, 1, 0)$ and $y^* = (0, 1, 1, 1, 1, 1, 1)$. The objective function is $C^* = 62$.

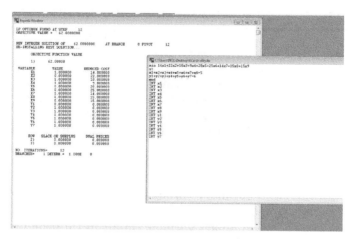

Figure 6.13. *Output of the LINDO optimizer for a k-cardinality problem with n = 7 and k = 5*

This solution is equivalent to the following graph:

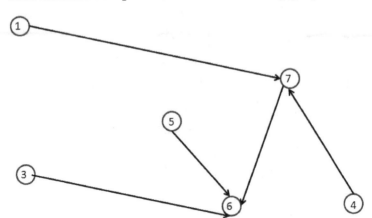

Figure 6.14. *The graph solution of the example of a k-cardinality problem with n = 7 and k = 5*

6.4.3. *Notation*

Following are the main symbols used to model the KCT problem:

Symbols	Explanation
G	A connected undirected weighted graph
V	Set of nodes $\{1, \ldots, n\}$
E	Set of edges $\{1, \ldots, m\}$
n	Number of nodes
m	Number of edges
K	Number of edges to attempt
W	Function cost associated to each edge e in E
w_e	The cost of edge e
V'	A subset of V
E'	A subset of E
x_e	A binary variable equals to 1 if the edge e in E'; 0 otherwise
y_i	A binary variable equals to 1 if node i is in V'
$E(V')$	$\{[i, j] \in E \mid i, j \in U\}$
T	A subgraph of G

6.4.4. *Mathematical formulation*

The mathematical formulation of the k-cardinality problem is as follows:

$$Min \ \sum_{e \in E} w_e x_e$$

$$S.t. \ \sum_{e \in E'} x_e = K$$

$$\sum_{i \in V'} y_i = K + 1$$

$$\sum_{e \in E(V')} x_e \leq \sum_{i \in V'} y_i - y_j \forall V' \subseteq V, |V'| \geq 2, j \in T \qquad [6.4]$$

$$x_e \in \{0,1\} \qquad\qquad \forall e \in U'$$

$$y_i \in \{0,1\} \qquad\qquad \forall i \in V'$$

The last constraint ensures the acyclicity since from all edges which have both endpoints in V' at most $|V| - 1$ can be chosen.

6.4.5. *Greedy approaches for the k-cardinality tree problem*

6.4.5.1. *The **k**-Prim approach and the dual-greedy algorithm*

The first greedy algorithm called the k-Prim approach consists of building n subtrees with k-cardinality starting each time by a node v of V.

Another greedy heuristic starts with the initial graph G by pruning edges in a greedy way until obtaining a tree with k-cardinality. The algorithm should verify in each iteration the connectivity of the graph.

Algorithm 17 The k-Prim algorithm

1: For every node $v \in V$

    – $V(T_v) \leftarrow \{v\}$

    – $E(T_v) \leftarrow \emptyset$

    – For $i = 1, ..., K$

      - Let $e \in E \backslash E(T_v)$ any edge with minimum weight such that $T_v \cup \{e\}$

      - $T_v \cup \{e\}$

2: $T_{heuristic} \leftarrow argmin\{w(T_v)|v = 1, ..., n\}$

Algorithm 18 The dual-greedy algorithm

1: $T \leftarrow G$

2: Repeat

    – Let e an edge $\in E(T)$ with a maximal weight such that $T \backslash \{e\}$ is connected and has at least $k + 1$ nodes.

    – $T \leftarrow T \backslash \{e\}$

    Until $|E(T)| = k$

3: $T_{heuristic} \leftarrow T$

6.4.6. *Minimum path approach*

A second class of heuristics is based on the minimum path approach. In fact, as the Dijkstra algorithm is for the minimum path problem, there is a k-Dijkstra for the k-MST problem. The Dijkstra algorithm computes for each node x a label $lab[x]$ which is the weight of minimum paths from the initial node s to x. The main loop of the algorithm chooses the node x with minimum label. For any node y adjacent to x, we try to see if the path containing x outperforms the path already found from s to y. If yes, then we update the $lab[y]$ by $min(lab[y], lab[x] + w(x, y))$ where $w(x, y)$ is the weight of the edge (x, y). The k-Dijkstra algorithm used to solve the k-cardinality problem defines $len[x]$ the number of edges of the best path from an initial node s to any node x.

6.4.7. *A genetic approach for the k-cardinality problem*

In this section we present a new approach using evolutionary operators but with no mutation. This approach is called the evolutionary computation. Christian Blum and Maria J. Blesa [BLU 05] presented this new approach to solve the k-cardinality problem. Their algorithm inspires us to present a solution for the k-cardinality problem.

Algorithm 19 An evolutionary algorithm for the k-cardinality problem

---

1: $n \leftarrow Determine\_Population\_Size$
2: $P \leftarrow Generate\_Initial\_Population(n)$
3: While (termination criterion not satisfied) Do

  – Crossover(P)

  – $Best\_Improvement\_Local\_Search(P)$

  – Update the best solution found S^*

  End while.

4: $S_{heuristic} \leftarrow S^*$

Blum and Blesa [BLU 05] suggest that the population's size is equal to $popsize = \lfloor |E|/k \rfloor$ with E being the set of edges. Then, we randomly generate an initial population P with size $popsize$. Each individual is a feasible KCT T_k having k edges. To apply the crossover, we have to choose two individuals from the population P which have at least one edge in common. The choice is made in a roulette wheel selection manner. Blum and Blesa [BLU 05] used a union-crossover, where edges that appear only in one of the two parents are preferred and an intersection-crossover, where edges that are common to both parents are preferred. The Figure 6.15 shows an example of how the crossover developed by Blum and Blesa [BLU 05] can perform two new individuals.

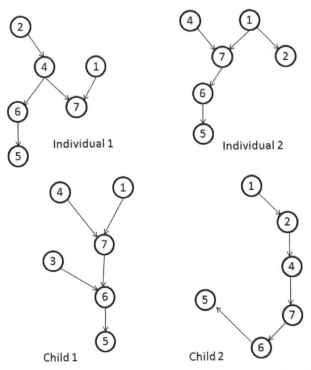

Figure 6.15. *An example of the crossover for the k-cardinality problem with $n = 7$ and $k = 5$*

6.5. The capacitated minimum spanning tree problem

6.5.1. *Problem definition*

Let $G = (V, E)$ be a valued connected graph with $V = \{0, 1, ..., n\}$ and E be the set of edges. Let node $r \in V$ be a central node. Each node $i \in V \setminus \{r\}$ has an associated demand d_i. To each edge $(i, j) \in E$ we associate a cost c_{ij}, and a capacity Q that limits the maximum flow on that edge. The CMST problem consists of finding a tree T from G with minimum cost, such that the sum of node demands in each connected part in T with $V \setminus \{r\}$ is less than or equal to Q. The CMST problem is *NP*-hard for $3 \leq Q \leq \frac{|V|}{2}$ [PAP 78].

6.5.2. *Notation*

Following are the main symbols used to model the CMST problem:

Symbols	Explanation
G	A connected undirected weighted graph
V	Set of nodes $\{1, \ldots, n\}$
E	Set of edges $\{1, \ldots, m\}$
n	Number of nodes
m	Number of edges
K	Number of disjoint subsets
W	Function cost associated to each edge e in E
w_e	The cost of edge e

A substantial body of research literature is devoted to the CMST problem. The survey paper by Gavish [GAV 91] gives a detailed understanding of telecommunication design problems where the CMST problem arises.

6.5.3. *An example*

The CMST problem is a fundamental problem in telecommunication network design. In this problem, we try to build a centralized network: we are given a central processor and a set of remote terminals with specified demands representing data traffic that must flow between the central processor and terminals. The objective is to build a minimum cost network to carry this demand. Between any pair of terminals or between the central processor and the terminals, there is a potential link that can be included for a given cost. The problem is to design a network connecting the central processor with terminals and having the following properties:

– the network is a tree;

– the sum of demands in each subtree defined by a group of terminals is less or equal to Q;

– the total cost of the network is minimal.

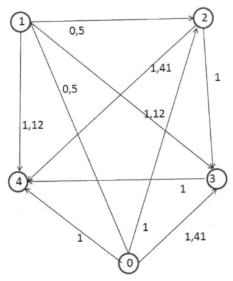

Figure 6.16. *An example of the capacitated minimum spanning tree problem*

6.5.4. *Solution approaches for the CMST problem*

6.5.4.1. *A greedy approach*

A greedy heuristic for the CMST problem starts with an empty spanning tree, and then adds edges in a greedy fashion based on a modified cost structure without violating the capacity constraint, until it finds a feasible spanning tree.

6.5.4.2. *Genetic algorithm for the CMST problem*

In this section, we will present a GA developed by Zhou and Gen [ZHO 03] and applied for the telecommunication network design problem.

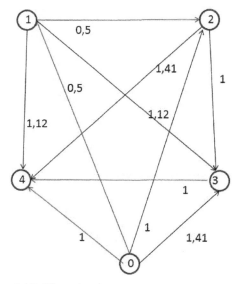

Figure 6.17. *The solution to the example of capacitated minimum spanning tree problem*

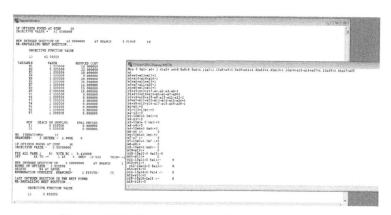

Figure 6.18. *The mathematical formulation of an example of CMST problem*

6.5.4.2.1. Encoding

The authors used the intuitive idea of encoding a tree solution by using a two-dimensional structure:

```
LP OPTIMUM FOUND AT STEP      53
OBJECTIVE VALUE =   3.61009860


LP OPTIMUM FOUND AT STEP      35
OBJECTIVE VALUE =   3.50000000

FIX ALL VARS.(    8)  WITH RC >  0.410000
SET         X4 TO >=    1 AT    1. BND=  -3.500      TWIN= -3.500        75

NEW INTEGER SOLUTION OF     3.50000000      AT BRANCH      1 PIVOT      75
BOUND ON OPTIMUM:  3.500000
DELETE        X4 AT LEVEL      1
ENUMERATION COMPLETE. BRANCHES=      1 PIVOTS=      75

LAST INTEGER SOLUTION IS THE BEST FOUND
RE-INSTALLING BEST SOLUTION...

          OBJECTIVE FUNCTION VALUE

      1)      3.500000

   VARIABLE          VALUE          REDUCED COST
        X1          0.000000          0.500000
        X2          0.000000          1.000000
        X3          0.000000          1.410000
        X4          1.000000          1.000000
        X5          1.000000          0.500000
        X6          1.000000          0.500000
        X7          0.000000          1.120000
        X8          0.000000          1.120000
        X9          0.000000          1.000000
       X10          1.000000          0.500000
       X11          0.000000          1.000000
       X12          0.000000          1.410000
       X13          0.000000          1.410000
       X14          0.000000          1.120000
       X15          0.000000          1.000000
       X16          0.000000          1.000000
       X17          0.000000          1.000000
       X18          0.000000          1.120000
       X19          0.000000          1.410000
       X20          1.000000          1.000000
        Y5          2.000000          0.000000
        Y9          0.000000          0.000000
       Y13          0.000000          0.000000
       Y17          0.000000          0.000000
        Y1          2.000000          0.000000
       Y10          1.000000          0.000000
       Y14          0.000000          0.000000
       Y18          0.000000          0.000000
        Y2          0.000000          0.000000
        Y6          2.000000          0.000000
       Y15          0.000000          0.000000
       Y19          0.000000          0.000000
        Y3          0.000000          0.000000
        Y7          0.000000          0.000000
       Y11          0.000000          0.000000
```

Figure 6.19. *The output of the example of the CMST problem on LINDO*

1) The first dimension encodes the nodes of a spanning tree.

2) The second one encodes the degree value of each node.

Therefore, each individual is a $2 \times n$ matrix where n is the number of nodes. The first row r_1 is an integer encoding where r_{1i} is equal to node i if this node is spanned by the tree.

The second row r_2 is also an integer encoding equal to the degree of each node chosen in r_1. We assume that node 1 is the root node and the first digit in the node dimension and its degree value as the first digit in the degree dimension. Zhou and Gen [ZHO 03] proved that this encoding is well adapted to the evolutionary process and thus adopted as the genetic representation for the CMST problem.

6.5.4.2.2. Fitness

It is important to point out that before computing the fitness function, Zhou and Gen [ZHO 03] proposed a procedure for decoding each individual using the following procedure:

Algorithm 20 A decoding procedure for an individual in GA for CMST problem

---

1: $N(i)$ with $i = 1, 2, ..., n$ the node dimension of individual i
2: $D(i)$ with $i = 1, 2, ..., n$ the degree dimension of individual i
3: $i = 1; j = 2$
4: Select the node $r = N(i)$ and the node $s = N(j)$; add the edge $r \to s$ into a tree.
5: $D(i) \leftarrow D(i) - 1$ and $D(j) \leftarrow D(j) - 1$.
6: If $D(i) = 0$ then $i \leftarrow i - 1$ otherwise go to 8.
7: If $(j = n)$ then STOP; otherwise go to 6.
8: If $D(j) \geq 1$ then:

   $- i \leftarrow j$

   $- j \leftarrow j + 1$

   $-$ Go to 2

   Otherwise $j \leftarrow j + 1$ and go to 4.

After applying this procedure, all generated individuals are feasible and their fitness is then computed as $\sum_{i=1}^{n-1} \sum_{j=2}^{n} c_{ij} x_{ij}$.

6.5.4.2.3. Mutation

In this version of GA, the authors used only the mutation operator with three variants:

1) Exchange mutation on nodes: randomly selects two positions in an individual and then swap the nodes.

2) Inversion mutation on nodes: randomly selects two nodes then inverts the substring between these two nodes.

3) Insertion mutation: randomly selects a subtree in an individual and inserts it in a random node.

We note here that if there are such individuals whose subtrees violate the capacity constraint, then we use the insertion mutation operation to insert the extra branch on a subtree into an other subtree with fewer nodes.

6.5.4.2.4. Parameters

The table below shows the parameters used for the GA to solve the CMST problem.

Parameters	Value
$Popsize$	200
Probability of mutation p_m	0.3
Number of generations	500
Number of iterations	20

6.6. Conclusion

This chapter has presented a fundamental problem of graph theory which is the minimum spanning tree problem. Then three combinatorial optimization problems based on spanning trees were detailed: the generalized minimum spanning tree problem, the k-cardinality problem and the capacitated minimum spanning tree problem. For each problem, we have stated its mathematical formulation, an illustrative example and two solution approaches based on the greedy algorithm and the genetic algorithm.

Steiner Problems

7.1. Introduction

In this chapter, we consider problems closely related to spanning tree problems but much more difficult. These problems are included in the class of Steiner problems in graphs. There are many variants of the Steiner problems depending on the nature of the graph. In fact, in the literature, there are three different variants of the Steiner problems:

– *Euclidean Steiner tree problem* where the graph is complete, straight lines are the edges and the distance between any two edges is Euclidean.

– *Rectilinear Steiner tree problem* where the graph is also complete and the distance $d(i, j)$ between two edges is rectilinear where $d(i, j) = |x_1 - x_2| + |y_1 - y_2|$ with $i(x_1, y_1)$ and $j(x_2, y_2)$.

– *Steiner tree problem on the graph* where we have any graph with edges and specific distances.

There are also many different problems using the general Steiner tree problem such as the prize collecting Steiner tree problem and the delay constrained Steiner tree problem. In this chapter, we will define each problem and will present its definition, its mathematical formulation and its resolution with greedy heuristics and with a genetic algorithm.

7.2. The Steiner tree problem

7.2.1. *Problem definition*

Let $G = (V, E)$ be an evaluated graph. Let T be a set of terminal nodes that should be connected. The Steiner problem consists of finding a tree of G containing all terminal nodes T with a minimum weight. The optimal tree can contain other nodes called *Steiner nodes* in the set $S = T \backslash V$. An example of the Steiner problem is presented in Figure 7.1. We note that two special cases of Steiner problem are solved polynomially:

– If $|T| = 2$, then the Steiner problem is equivalent to the shortest path.

– If $T = V$, then the Steiner problem is equivalent to the minimum spanning tree problem.

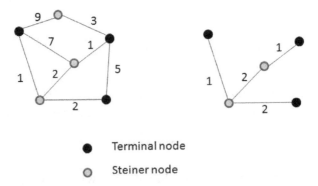

●   Terminal node

○   Steiner node

Figure 7.1. *An example of the Steiner tree problem*

However, in the general case, the Steiner tree problem is *NP*-hard [GAR 79].

7.2.2. *Problem formulation*

Let a graph be $G = (V, E)$ where V is the set of nodes and E is the set of edges. We define $T \subset V$ as the set of terminal nodes and $S = V \backslash T$ as the set of Steiner nodes. Then, the Steiner tree problem is stated as:

$$Min \quad C(x) = \sum_{e \in E} w_e x_e$$

$$S.t. \text{ to } \sum_{e \in \delta(S)} x_e \geq 1 \text{for } S \subset V \text{with } S \cap T \neq \emptyset, T \backslash S \neq \emptyset,$$

$$\text{and } x_e \in \{0, 1\} \text{for } e \in E$$

[7.1]

7.2.3. *Constructive heuristics for the Steiner tree problem*

7.2.3.1. *Shortest paths heuristic*

Let a graph be $G = (V, E)$ where V is the set of n nodes, E is the set of edges and $T = \{1, ..., p\}$ is the set of terminal nodes (there are p terminal nodes). Takashi and Matsuyama [TAK 80] suggested the following heuristic.

The complexity of this heuristic is $O(pn^2)$ as we do p shortest paths with at most $O(n^2)$.

7.2.3.2. *Shortest distance heuristic*

Another heuristic using the shortest path is the shortest distance heuristic detailed as follows.

This heuristic was tested on problems with 100 nodes and 500 edges. The average gap is about 3.9%. On 19 test problems, this greedy heuristic gave only five times the best solution.

Algorithm 21 Shortest paths heuristic for the Steiner tree problem

---

1: Randomly choose one terminal node from T. Let this first subtree ST_1.

2: $k \leftarrow 1$ and $ST_k \leftarrow \{i\}$.

3:    – Find a terminal node $i \in T \backslash T_k$ (T_k is a subset of T) the nearest to ST_k

   – Build a subtree ST_{k+i} by adding the cost of the shortest path between i and ST_k

   – $k \leftarrow k + 1$

4: If $k < p$ then go to Step 2. If $k = p$ then return ST_p as solution and stop.

Algorithm 22 Shortest distance heuristic for the Steiner tree problem

---

1: Build a complete graph G' with the whole set of terminal nodes and assign to each edge in G', the cost of the shortest path between any two nodes.

2: Find a minimum spanning tree ST on the graph G'

3: Replace each edge in ST by the corresponding shortest path and obtain $ST = (V_{ST}, E_{ST})$.

4:    – Find a minimum spanning tree $ST' = (V'_{ST}, E'_{ST})$.

   – While there is a leaf in ST', which is a Steiner node, then delete this leaf and all its incident edges.

5: Delete from ST' all edges and Steiner nodes such that:

   – there is no cycle;

   – all remaining leaves are terminal nodes.

6: Return ST'

7.2.3.3. *Arbitrary node insertion*

This greedy heuristic gives a maximal deviation of 54% and an average deviation of 5.12%. In 33.76%, it gives the best solution [TAK 80].

Algorithm 23 Arbitrary node insertion for the Steiner tree problem

---

1: T =one terminal node Randomly chosen.
2: Repeat until T has all terminal nodes:
   - Choose arbitrary a node p^* not in V_T.
   - Find the nearest node $v^* \in V_T$ and add the edge (v^*, p^*) to T.
3: Return T

7.2.3.4. *Cheapest node insertion*

Algorithm 24 Cheapest node insertion for the Steiner tree problem

---

1: $T = \{w\}$ where w is one terminal node chosen randomly.
2: Repeat until T contains all terminal nodes:
   - Find two nodes v^* and p^* the nearest to w where $v^* \in V_T$ and p^* not in V_T.
   - Add the edge (v^*, p^*) to T.
3: Return T

This heuristic gives a maximal deviation of 15.07% and an average deviation of 1%. In 46.81% it gives the best solution.

7.2.3.5. *Cheapest node insertion for all roots*

Algorithm 25 Node cheapest insertion for all roots

1: Apply the heuristic "cheapest node insertion" for each terminal node with which we start.
2: Choose among all trees obtained in step1, the cheapest solution.

This heuristic gives a maximal deviation of 6.98% and an average deviation of 0.2%. In 84.65% of cases, it gives the best known solution.

7.3. The price collecting Steiner tree problem

7.3.1. *Problem definition*

Let a graph be $G = (V, E)$ where:

$- V$ is the set of nodes containing, T is the set of terminal nodes;

$- E$ is the set of edges with a non-negative edge weight w_e;

$-$ a non-negative prize p_j associated with each node $j \in V$;

$-$ a specified root node 1;

$-$ a preset prize quota Q.

The prize collecting Steiner tree problem (PCSTP) is to find a minimum cost tree T including a subset of terminal nodes $ST \subset V$ with root node 1 such that the sum of nodes' prize of ST is at least equal to Q.

7.3.2. *Example*

Let us consider Figure 7.2 where we have a graph with 17 nodes. Numbers on the edges are the weights and those below the nodes are the prizes. The preset quota is $Q = 40$. The solution of the example is in Figure 7.3.

7.3.3. *Mathematical formulation*

In this section, we present a mathematical formulation developed by [HAO 06] for the PCSTP using the minimum spanning tree with constraints. For that let us consider a graph $G = (V, E)$ where:

– V is the set of nodes containing, T is the set of terminal nodes;

– E is the set of edges with a non-negative edge weight w_e;

– a non-negative prize p_j associated with each node $j \in V$;

– a specified root node 1;

– and a preset prize quota Q.

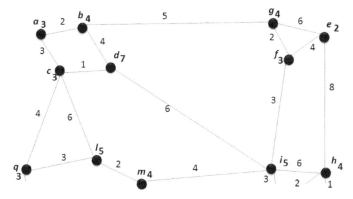

Figure 7.2. *An example of the prize collecting Steiner tree problem*

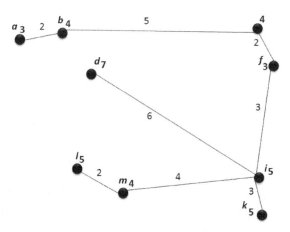

Figure 7.3. *A feasible solution of the example of the prize collecting Steiner tree problem where $Q = 40$*

Now, consider a new graph $G' = (V', E')$ where we add a dummy node 0 and edges of the form $(0, j)$ for every $j \in V$. These edges have a zero weight. Let $T = (V', E'(T))$ a spanning tree of G' and V_0 the set of adjacent nodes to 0. In fact, if T satisfies the following conditions:

– The node 1 is connected to the dummy node 0.

– All nodes except node 1 in V_0 have a degree equal to 1.

– Let $\overline{Q} = \sum_{j \in V} p_j - Q$, then the total prizes of all nodes in V_0 is less than $\overline{Q}$.

Then, by removing node 0 and all its adjacent edges, the resulting graph is a feasible PCSTP solution. Therefore, an integer programming formulation for the PCSTP is as follows:

$$Min \quad \sum_{(i,j) \in E'} c_{ij} x_{ij}$$

$S.t.\text{to} \ x_{01} = 1$

$$x_{0j} + x_{ij} \leq 1 \qquad\qquad j \in V \backslash \{1\}, \{i, j\} \in E \quad [7.2]$$

$$\sum_{j \in V \backslash \{1\}} p_j x_{0j} \leq \overline{Q}$$

x_{ij} defines a spanning tree on G'

7.3.4. A greedy approach to solve the PCSTP

In this section we present a simple greedy-type heuristic, which is an extension of the Prim algorithm – we call it a "modified Prim heuristic". It starts from root 1 and then connects to a node that minimizes a ratio f_j equal to the minimum cost of adjacent nodes to j divided by the prize p_j of node j. The algorithm stops when the constraint of quota is satisfied. However, we can improve this solution by building a minimum spanning tree on nodes found in the obtained feasible solution and then proceed to node pruning to remove all unnecessary leaves.

Algorithm 26 A modified Prim heuristic for the PCSTP

1: Initialization $S \leftarrow \{1\}$, $q \leftarrow 0$, $V' \leftarrow V\backslash\{1\}$.
2: Node selection while $(q < Q)$ do:

  – For all $j \in V'$, compute $f_j = \frac{min_{i \in S} c_{ij}}{p_j}$.
  – Let $k = argmin_{j \in V'}(f_j)$.
  – Set $S \leftarrow S \cup \{k\}$.
  – Set $q \leftarrow q + p_k$.
  – Set $V' \leftarrow V'\backslash\{k\}$.

  End while.
3: Find the minimum weight tree T spanning the subset S using the Prim algorithm.
4: Node Pruning:

  – Let $P = \{j \in S\backslash\{1\} : j$ is a leaf of T and $q - p_j \geq Q\}$.
  – For each $j \in P$, let γ_j the weight of the edge adjacent to j.
  – If $P = \emptyset$, then STOP. Else:
    - Set $S = S\backslash\{k\}$ where $k = argmax_{j \in P}(\gamma_j)$.
    - Go to Step 4.

The computing time of this greedy heuristic is the same as the Prim algorithm.

7.3.5. A genetic algorithm for the PCSTP

In this section, we present a simple version of the genetic algorithm rather than the version developed by Haouari and Chaouachi [HAO 06], which is well-developed and includes Lagrangian information to compute the fitness using reduced costs and also an evolutionary algorithm as a mutation operator. However, we will use the same encoding and crossover operator.

7.3.5.1. *Encoding*

Each individual is represented by a binary string $s = (s_2, s_3, ..., s_n)$ of length $|V| - 1$ where $s_i = 1$ if the node i is in the feasible PCSTP, 0 otherwise.

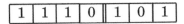

7.3.5.2. *Fitness*

We use the modified Prim procedure to compute the fitness of any individual. Therefore, we guarantee the feasibility of all individuals in the population and consequently there is no need for penalization or reparation strategy.

7.3.5.3. *Crossover*

We use a two-point crossover for recombination strategy as shown in the figure below:

| 1 | 1 || 0 | 1 || 1 | 0 | 1 |

| 1 | 0 || 1 | 1 || 0 | 1 | 1 |

The new chromosomes obtained, whenever the second and the fourth positions are the crossover points, are:

| 1 | 0 | 0 | 1 | 0 | 1 | 1 |

| 1 | 1 | 1 | 1 | 1 | 0 | 1 |

The results of a computational study show that the modified Prim heuristic is very fast but gives a deviation ranging from 1.61% to 49.82%. However, the genetic algorithm requires a relatively long computing time yet yields to near optimal solutions (less than 2%). Haouari and Chaouachi [HAO 06] reported that the instances tend to get harder as the quota gets smaller.

7.4. Conclusion

In this chapter, we presented another fundamental problem of graph theory which is the Steiner Tree problem. For this problem, many constructive heuristics were detailed with examples. Then the Prize-Collecting Steiner Tree Problem (PCST) was defined and solved using a greedy approach and a genetic algorithm.

8

A DSS Design for Optimization Problems

8.1. Introduction

Decision support systems (DSSs) are large-scaled platforms that generally dispose of a set of information helping decision makers (DMs) to take a rational decision for complex structured problems. It consists of iterative interactions with the DM that will provide preference levels in order to tighten the search space. The optimization of the decision level in a reasonable time interval makes the convergence to an individual or a group decision very compromising. Each DSS disposes of two main components that are iteratively performed to make the application converge to the area of interest:

– *Interactive phase:* in which the system collects all the information that helps the generation of additional solutions. Such information can be thresholds for the objective to be reached, or other structural requirements in the set of constraints. All such data are merged and translated quantatively in order to become inputs for the calculation phase.

– *Calculation phase:* during the problem, the statement is updated according to the additional information. Based on the new modeling, solution approaches are adopted to solve the problem and generate a candidate solution to be evaluated in later stages by the DM.

A DSS is qualified as a material for the rational decision-making whose quality output depends on the accuracy of the input data. We propose, in the present chapter, to define the DSS and its architecture and usefulness in handling optimization problems. We stress our analysis on DSSs for the routing and benefits in displaying and interpreting cost-saving pathways generated by concurrential solution approaches. We show, through a succession of interfaces, a DSS design that handles some optimization problems, namely the knapsack problem (KP) and the vehicle routing problem (VRP). We address the specific case of the VRP, an extensively studied optimization problem that finds its application in numerous applications. The DSS devoted to the VRP has the ability to make numerous solution approaches operational in order to be run in accordance with an information system that guides the search in terms of the capability of each approach in solving the configuration of the VRP being processed.

8.2. Definition of a DSS

The interactive decision support systems (IDSSs) "are computing systems providing assistance in the process of decision making".

The IDSS can be defined as "interactive information systems, flexible and adaptable, specially developed to quickly provide the decision makers of companies with the relevant information, enabling them to make better decisions in order to solve their management problems".

The support provided by the system can provide an episode of the decision that takes place:

– in a more productive way (i.e. faster, less expensive, with less effort);

– with greater agility (i.e. mental alertness to the unexpected ability);

– innovative (i.e. with a better idea, creativity, novelty, surprise);

– reputation (i.e. with excellent accuracy, ethics, quality, trust);

– with greater satisfaction with the decision-making actors (i.e. the participants of the decision, sponsors decision, consumers of the decision, implementors decision).

8.3. Taxonomy of a DSS

A DSS is, in most cases, made up of the following main components:

1) A language system: that details all messages that the DSS can handle and answer.

2) A presentation system: that reports all messages that can be sent by the DSS.

3) A knowledge system: that contains all inference rules and past recorded information that can be relevant for future deductions and interpretations of the problem results and expected events.

4) A problem processing system: that constitutes the kernel of the DSS. It encompasses all the solution approaches that help to solve the problem under study. As DSS should provide the most promising solution under the predefined framework, input parameters are very informative about the quality of the results generated. The operational process of a DSS starts by interacting with the users belonging to different hierarchical levels. Generally, the team of users is made of the DM, the

facilitator, and some other involved persons to explain some technical steps.

Before introducing the concept of IDSS, we will define some terminology.

Decision maker:

The decision maker can be responsible for an organization or is responsible of a function of this organization. He is also called a user.

Decision:

The decision is the selection of a choice among several solutions when solving a problem or a situation that we are facing.

8.4. Architecture and design of a DSS

To design a DSS, some methodologies are used, in this section, we will focus on those provided by Sotiris.

The main steps of the methodology used are:

– *Data collection:* all necessary data concerning the constraints, empirical optimization rules and infrastructure of information systems are collected.

– *Modeling of the distribution system:* this step is based on the analysis using modeling tools such as flow charts for functions and activities, flow diagrams of data for databases and information flows.

– *Research of market software:* the research of the international software market is the second procedure to examine the appropriate solutions for the management and distribution and specifically automation and optimization process of shipping company.

– *Specifications of system conditions:* after the completion of the research of the market software, a list of devices of the most specialized software concerning the current problem is deployed. From this list, the system requirements are extracted in the format of the criteria catalog of a choice.

– *Choice of software:* the criteria of catalog are sent to prequalified software companies such as requests for proposals (RFPs). The company receives all proposals and after evaluation, the most appropriate solutions are selected.

– *Implementation of the new system:* the software applications selected are integrated to implement DSSs. The case of development fully adapted to the appropriate customer needs has been thoroughly examined, and it was unacceptable because of high costs and extended time horizon. However, independently of the step of selecting a software, other methodological steps have been possible to be identical for the adapted customized software development.

8.4.1. *Architecture of a DSS*

Sotiris [SOT 11] has provided a design methodology for a DSS, reported in Figure 8.1, that shows the following succession of steps: the system architecture includes a central database managed by three main phases:

– The main inputs: they correspond to the available resources involved in the decision taking process.

– The planning and scheduling module: it is the calculation phase that applies optimization tools.

– The output of the generated results to be evaluated by the DM.

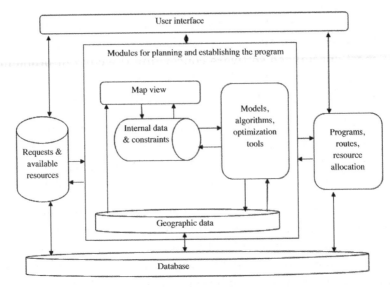

Figure 8.1. *DSS architecture*

8.4.2. *DSS design*

In this section we explain the different screenshots that can be of relevance in the design of a DSS for optimization problems, namely the KP and the CVRP. The first screenshot outputs the first interface for the DSS:

– *Interface 1* the start button of the first interface reported in Figure 8.2 allows the choice of the optimization problem to be solved.

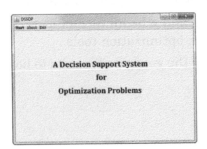

Figure 8.2. *The first interface of the DSS*

— Interface 2 this information interface outlined in Figure 8.3 enumerates some practical situations for both optimization problems.

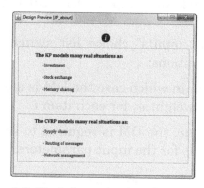

Figure 8.3. *The information interface of the DSS for KP and DCVRP*

8.5. A DSS for the knapsack problem

— Interface KP-1   The first interface for the KP-DSS, pointed out in Figure 8.4, requires the DM to input the problem parameters, namely:

Figure 8.4. *The information interface of the DSS for the KP*

– The first line records the number of items (n) from which a subset should be packed.

– The second line inputs the capacity (C) of the knapsack.

– The "Data inputs" choice list switches between the following two options:

- *Manual:* in which case the DM is asked to provide a profit p_i and a weight w_i for each item i.

- *Automatic:* the DM is required to specify profit and weight intervals for the input parameters.

– The "Next" button makes the DM move to the input interface of the other problem parameters and the resolution alternatives.

– *Interface KP-2:*   The second interface of the KP-DSS belonging to Figure 8.5 inputs the profit and weight parameters. Using such data, the problem formulation is stated using the "Generate instance" button.

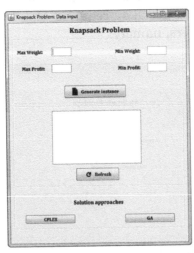

Figure 8.5. *The information interface of the DSS for the KP*

Two alternative solution approaches are available:

– *CPLEX optimizer:* this can operate only for limited sizes of the KP instances, due to the *NP*-hardness of the problem.

– *GA:* a genetic algorithm specifically implemented for the KP, as detailed in Chapter 2.

The solution is finally output to report the objective function value as well as the the binary vector of decision variables.

8.6. A DSS for the DCVRP

The use of DSS for solving optimization problems is important, as it facilitates the interaction with the system parameters and the input of the DM's preferences.

In this vein, Sotiris [SOL 11] enumerated the following benefits for the DSS:

– reducing the total transportation cost;

– improving fleet utilization of 11% and consequently fixed costs of vehicles. Reducing the required number of leased vehicles means minimizing costs of the leased fleet. The estimated savings due to the better utilization of the fleet are around 40,000 euros around per year;

– the savings of the reduction of staff for the order receiving and shipping estimate are 390,000 euros per year in the case of decentralized distribution (45% fewer personnel) and 700,000 euros per year for a central system (80% less personnel);

– more efficient processes that reduce the execution time for the shipping process and few errors (<1%), which involve the improvement of customer service. The calculated profit of the company is 250,000 euros per year.

Firstly, we state the DCVRP, a well-known optimization problem, that has been extensively studied in the literature, as it models a wide variety of practical applications in the routing of goods as well as in the routing of messages. In the second step, we explain the architecture of a personalized DSS, termed DCVRP–DSS, which handles the problem from the outputting of problem data untill the solution. As shown in Faiz and Krichen [FAI 13], the routing problem can be handled by an integrated system merging a geographic information system (GIS) and the optimization engine. We illustrate our purpose with a real example which takes the north west of Tunis as the area of interest.

In the mid-1960s, VRP solutions were based on non-automated methods, where routes were designed manually using paper cards that provided locations of customers to serve as geographic reference points.

In the early 1970s, some vehicle routing heuristics were used to generate routes with manual intervention accomplished by decision makers who had considerable knowledge of the local state and of the relative importance of various constraints.

From the early 1980s, each vehicle routing system (VRS) was seen as an IDSS, viewing its relationship with the management system database to organize the large amounts of data (customer orders, size of the vehicle fleet, etc.) and the use of a visual interface required to support a specific decision problem.

This problem attracted the attention of many researchers for many years, Tarantil is [TAR 02] introduced an architecture of a DSS for vehicle routing encompassing:

- a geographic information system (GIS);
- a management system database (DBMS);
- a network analysis tool (NAT);
- an optimization of vehicle routing problem tool (VROT);
- a user interface.

The GISs: these are characterized by interactive communication with management system databases and individual software that performs all necessary numerical calculations, and any cartographic and graphic load connected to a VRP.

Management system database: this is the heart of the DSS having a double role. In its social infrastructure, regional and operational data spatial and non-spatial related to the deposit and clients with their addresses as well as road maps and transport facilities in the region are stored.

The NAT: determines the shortest path, expressed in terms of distance traveled in a specific way.

The VROT: determines the best routing plan while minimizing the total distance traveled by the vehicle.

The user interface: is the only visible module by the user allowing us to act with the data and methods used to solve the VRP.

8.6.1. *Statement and modeling of the CVRP*

The CVRP consists of finding least cost routes for a heterogeneous fleet of vehicles that schedule their departures from a single depot to a set of geographically dispersed selling points. Each customer disposes of his specific demand to be delivered by one of the vehicles.

The CVRP, expressed as a connected graph $G = (V, E)$ such that:

– V: is the set of selling points and the depot.

– E: expresses the distances of direct routes between each pair of connected vertices.

The CVRP, designed as a connected graph, is reported in Figure 8.6.

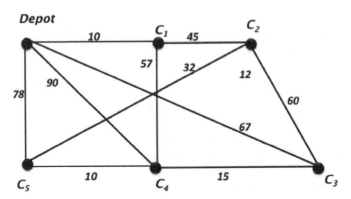

Figure 8.6. *Graph modeling of the CVRP*

Where $|V| = 6$ and $|E| = \frac{\sum_{i=1}^{6} deg(i)}{2} = \frac{4+3+3+3+4+3}{2} = 10$ edges. On the basis of the previously discussed statements, the textual formulation of the CVRP is written as follows:

Min the total travelling cost
S.t.

    −Each customer is served by exactly one vehicle
    −Each route starts and ends at the depot   [8.1]
    −The weight and distance capacity of each vehicle
    should be respected

As a first step, customers' demands and locations are specified in order to extract the required input data. Subsequently, customers' locations as well as the distance matrix are determined in order to obtain the corresponding graph. Once the transport network is created, the third step consists of choosing the cost saving vehicles depending on the total distance and the quantity of goods. The fourth step is about a cargo loading in which a set of orders has to be loaded in the chosen subset of vehicles. At the last step, each vehicle has its own pathway, and the loaded goods are delivered to the corresponding customers. We report hereby the main symbols used for the modeling of the VRP.

8.6.2. Notation

Following are the symbols used for the mathematical formulation of the DCVRP:

SYMBOLS	EXPLANATION
n	The total number of vehicles
m	The total number of customers
$V = \{0, \dots, m\}$	The set of vertices where 0 refers to the depot
$E = \{\{i,j\} : i, j \in V\}$	The set of edges
w_j	The order weight of customer j
c_{ij}^k	The traveling cost from i to j by vehicle k
$[w_{min}^k, w_{max}^k]$	The range of weight capacity for vehicle k
$[d_{min}^k, d_{max}^k]$	The distance range that vehicle k can travel

8.6.3. *Mathematical formulation of the DCVRP*

Based on the above mentioned assumptions in model [8.1], the mathematical formulation of the VRP with vehicles' weight and distance capacities is written as follows:

$$Min \ Z(x) = \sum_{i=1}^{n} \sum_{j=1}^{n} \sum_{k=1}^{v} c_{ij}^{k} x_{ij}^{k}$$

$S.t.$

$$\sum_{j=1}^{m} x_{0j}^{k} = 1 \quad k = 1, ..., m$$

$$\sum_{i=1}^{m} x_{i0}^{k} = 1 \quad k = 0, ..., m$$

$$\sum_{i=0}^{m} \sum_{k=1}^{n} \sum_{i \neq j, j=0}^{max} x_{ij}^{k} = 1 \ j = 1, ..., n \qquad [8.2]$$

$$\sum_{i=0}^{m} x_{ij}^{k} - \sum_{i=0}^{m} x_{ji}^{k} = 1, \ j = 1, ..., n, \ k = 1, ..., m$$

$$\sum_{i \in S} \sum_{j \in S} x_{ij}^{k} \leq |S| - 1, k = 1, ..., m, \forall S \subseteq V, |S| \in \{2, ..., n\}$$

$$w_{min}^{k} y^{k} \leq \sum_{i=0}^{m} \sum_{j \neq i, j=0}^{m} w_{j} x_{ij}^{k} \leq w_{max}^{k} y^{k}, \ k = 1, ..., m$$

$$d_{min}^{k} y^{k} \leq \sum_{i=0}^{m} \sum_{j \neq i, j=0}^{m} d_{ij} x_{ij}^{k} \leq d_{max}^{k} y^{k}, \ k = 1, ..., m$$

$$x_{ij}^{k}, y^{k} \in \{0, 1\}, i = 0, ..., n, \ j = 1, ..., n, \ k = 1, ..., m$$

– The objective function of the CVRP model [8.2] tries to minimize the total routing cost.

– The first set of constraints of [8.2] expresses that each traveling should start and end at the depot.

– The second set of constraints in the optimization model [8.2] guarantees that each customer is served by exactly one vehicle.

– The third set of requirements corresponds to the typical flow conservation equation that ensures the continuity of each vehicle's route.

– The subtour elimination is presented by the fourth set of constraints.

– The maximum capacity of a vehicle as well as its traveled distance belongs to an allowed range, as reported, respectively, in the last set of constraints of model [8.2].

We propose in what follows the DSS for handling the DCVRP that can operate either in simulation framework or using a real mapping area.

8.6.4. *DCVRP–DSS interfaces*

In urban public transport systems, there is often a set of information that is correlated and necessary for determining a decision. Taking a decision here is a complex process to select a choice between several solutions in which each process produces a final choice that can be an action or an opinion of choice.

More recently, new factors have emerged to make the position of enterprises more and more difficult to a global economic ladder.

Therefore to avoid this limitation, each company tries to adopt a strategy that ensures continuous exploitation of information, as well as an optimization of the decision-making level within an acceptable time period, in order to build the DSS. However, the work done is an optimization of time and costs by adapting the DSS on the real site. The latter has been done for the city of Jendouba.

In what follows we detail the main interface steps that characterize a DCVRP–DSS:

– *Interface DCVRP-1*: The first interface requires the DM to enter his routing input data. Figure 8.7 describes the required information for a good definition of the routing instance. A list of customers is then displayed from which the DM has to select those to be included in the currently handled routing problem. For each selected customer, a specific demand is entered.

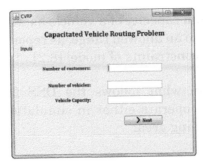

Figure 8.7. *The DCVRP-DSS applied to the north west of Tunisia*

– *Interface DCVRP-2*: If a new customer is to be input, the system will require its geographical coordinates by locating it using a geographical tool. Alternatively, a new vehicle followed by its specific features can be appended to the set of available vehicles. Once a vehicle's data have entered, the system outputs a confirmation icon as shown in Figure 8.8.

Figure 8.8. *The insertion of a new customer in the DCVRP–DSS*

– *Interface DCVRP-3*: After specifying the set of customers and the set of available vehicles, the application proceeds by making the DM choose the appropriate solution approach and the waiting time for generating the solution. The numerical solution is then displayed as shown in Figure 8.9.

To operationalize the benefits of using a DSS for routing problem variants in a more concrete way, we develop a real application that schedules in the next section.

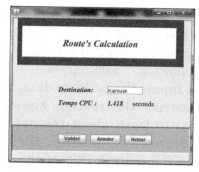

Figure 8.9. *The DCVRP–DSS applied to the north west of Tunisia*

8.6.5. A real application: the case of Tunisia

In this section, we address the specific area of the north west of Tunisia shown in Figure 8.10. The depot and the set of customers are located in the considered zone, and the DCVRP–DSS tries to satisfy the customers' demands, corresponding passengers' transportation to their destinations.

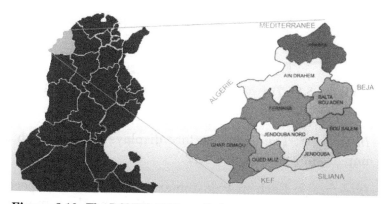

Figure 8.10. *The DCVRP–DSS applied to the north west of Tunisia*

The problem consists of scheduling buses to which departures are planned from a central depot to intermediate points. The pathway and the number of buses used are scheduled in terms of the number of passengers for each destination. Each bus disposes of a fixed number of seats, and cannot exceed a predetermined travel distance. Taking into account the following assumptions, we develop a DCVRP–DSS that inputs the problem data. Then, a database system tries to extract the routing knowledge about the mentioned problem to learn about the appropriate solution approach to be adopted. We describe, thereafter, the main steps that describe the routing DSS of the transportation of passengers:

– *Interface 1*: The system proceeds by determining the destination knowing that the central departure point is the city of "Jendouba", as shown in Figure 8.11.

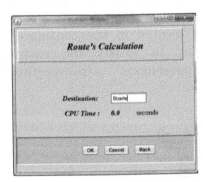

Figure 8.11. *The calculation of the best path using the GA*

– *Interface 2*: The next interface displays the bus' path on the map as shown in Figure 8.12.

– *Interface 3*: Each new customer is assigned to a specific vehicle taking into account his destination and the remaining number of places in the currently handled bus, as presented in Figure 8.13.(a).

Once the bus becomes full, a new bus is used to assign new arriving customers (see Figure 8.13.(b)).

Figure 8.12. *The calculation of the best path using the GA*

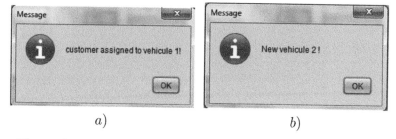

$a)$ $b)$

Figure 8.13. *Customers' management for the routing of passengers*

8.7. Conclusion

We have provided the design of a DSS for two well-known optimization problems, namely the KP and the VRP. For the KP, the problem starts by asking the DM for problem data inputs. Then, the application offers the DM an opportunity to solve the problem either by the CPLEX optimizer that generates the optimal solution or by applying the GA in order to approximate the optimal solution. These information systems facilitating the process of decision support can take many forms ranging from the executive information systems (EISs) providing the useful information to the decision maker, to executive support systems (ESSs) to analyze the data and obtain an estimate of the future of the organization, through the IDSS providing directly relevant information to the decision maker to solve the problems of decision-making. This chapter has shown that despite the difficulties encountered in its implementation, DSS is still a valuable contribution that requires the gain of time and money.

Conclusion

In this book, we have provided an overview on optimization problems that can be designed as a graph. We started by stating the more generic problem, called the knapsack problem (KP) as it is known to be able to model all other optimization problems.

To continue studying in the framework of packing, we moved to the bin packing problem and its variants and exposed most of its variants. We showed that the class of packing problems are modeled as bipartite graphs. The assignment and scheduling problems are also good examples for a graph-related illustration. For each problem, we devoted a whole chapter to explore its features and solution approaches in more detail. Tree-based problems, called spanning tree and Steiner tree problems well operationalize the utilization of a graph representation. Our book is enclosed by the design of a decision support system that can handle an optimization problem as the KP or the routing problem. We illustrated our proposal by the real application a routing of passengers within the north west of Tunisia.

Glossary

KP	*Knapsack problem*
QKP	*Quadratic knapsack problem*
ST	*Steiner tree*
AP	*Assignment problem*
AP	*Bin packing problem*
GA	*Genetic algorithm*
RCPSP	*Resource constrained project scheduling problem*
DSS	*Decision support system*
MST	*Minimum Spanning Tree*
KCT	*K Cardinality Tree*
CMST	*Capacitated Minimum Spanning Tree*
GMST	*Generalized Minimum Spanning Tree*
EGMST	*Exact Generalized Minimum Spanning Tree*
PCST	*Prize Collecting Steiner Tree*
ST	*Steiner Tree*

Bibliography

[AHU 03] AHUJA R.K., ORLIN J.B., SHARMA D., "A positive very large-scale neighborhood structure for the capacitated minimum spanning tree problem", *Operations Research Letters*, vol. 31, pp. 185–194, 2003.

[ANS 12] ANSTREICHER K.M., "Interior-point algorithms for a generalization of linear programming and weighted centring", *Optimization Methods and Software*, vol. 27, no. 4–5, pp. 605–612, 2012.

[BLA 83] BLAZEWIEZ J., LENSTRA J.K., RINNOOY KAN A.H.G., "Scheduling subject to resource constraints: classification and complexity", *Discrete Applied Mathematics*, vol. 5, pp. 11–24, 1983.

[BLU 05] BLUM C., BLESA M.J., "New metaheuristic approaches for the edge-weighted k-cardinality tree problem", *Computers and Operations Research,* vol. 32, no. 6, pp. 1355–1377, 2005.

[BOR 97] BORND NORFER R., FERREIRA C., MARTIN A., Matrix decomposition by branch-and-cut, Technical Report, Konrad Zuse Center for Information Technology, Berlin, 1997.

[BOR 98] BORND NORFER R., FERREIRA C., Martin A., "Decomposing matrices into blocks", *SIAM Journal on Optimization,* vol. 9, no. 1, pp. 236–269, 1998.

[BUR 11] BURGER M., NOTARSTEFANO G., BULLO F., *et al.*, "A distributed simplex algorithm for degenerate linear programs and multi-agent assignment", *Automatica*, vol. 48, no. 9, pp. 2298–2304, 2011.

[CHA 73] CHANDY K.M., LO T., "The capacitated minimum spanning tree", *Networks*, vol. 3, pp. 173–182, 1973.

[CHE 94] CHEUNG S.Y., KUMAR A., "ELcient quorumcast routing algorithms", *Proceedings of INFOCOM'94*, Los Alamitos, CA, IEEE Society Press, Silver Spring, MD, 1994.

[COO 11] COOK W., KOCH T., DANIEL E., *et al.*, "An exact rational mixed-integer programming solver", *Proceedings of the 15th International Conference on Integer Programming and Combinatoral Optimization, IPCO11*, Springer-Verlag, Berlin, Heidelberg, pp. 104–116, 2011.

[DAM 06] DAMMAK A., ELLOUMI A., KAMOUN H., "Classroom assignment for exam timetabling", *Advances in Engineering Software*, vol. 37, pp. 659–666, 2006.

[DEN 11] DENG G.F., LIN W.T., "Ant colony optimization-based algorithm for airline crew scheduling problem", *Expert Systems with Applications*, vol. 38, pp. 5787–5793, 2011.

[DOR 00a] DROR M., HAOUARI M., CHAOAUCHI J., "Generalized spanning trees", *European Journal of Operational Research*, vol. 120, pp. 583–592, 2000.

[DOR 00b] DROR M., HAOUARI M., "Generalized Steiner problems and other variants", *Journal of Combinatorial Optimization*, vol. 4, no. 4, pp. 415–436, 2000.

[DRI 12] DRIDI O., KRICHEN S., GUITOUNI A., "A multi-objective optimization approach for resource assignment and task scheduling problem: application to maritime domain awareness", *IEEE World Congress on Computational Intelligence (WCCI)*, pp. 1–8, 2012.

[FAI 13] FAIZ S., KRICHEN S., *Geographical Information Systems and Spatial Optimization*, Taylor & Francis Editions, U. (ed.), Science Publisher, 2013.

[FOU 92] FOULDS L.R., HAMACHER H.W., A new integer programming approach to (restricted) facilities layout problems allowing flexible facility shapes, Technical Report no. 1992-3, Department of Management Science, University of Waikato, 1992.

[FOU 98] FOULDS L.R., HAMACHER H.W., WILSON J., "Integer programming approaches to facilities layout models with forbidden areas", *Annals of Operations Research*, vol. 81, pp. 405–417, 1998.

[GAL 80] GALLO G., HAMMER P., SIMEONE B., "Quadratic knapsack problems", *Mathematical Programming Study*, vol. 12, pp. 132–149, 1980.

[GAR 77] GAREY M.R., JOHNSON D.S., "The rectilinear Steiner problem is NP-complete", *SIAM Journal on Applied Mathematics*, vol. 32, pp. 826–834, 1977.

[GAR 79a] GAREY M.R., JOHNSON D.S., *Computers and Intractability*, W.H. Freemann, New York, NY, 1979.

[GAR 79b] GAREY M.R., JOHNSON D.S., *Computers and Intractability: A Guide to the Theory of NP-Completeness* (Series of Books in the Mathematical Sciences), W. H. Freeman, 1979.

[GAR 97] GARG N., HOCHBAUM D., "An O(log k) approximation algorithm for the k minimum spanning tree problem in the plane", *Algorithmica*, vol. 18, no. 1, pp. 111–121, 1997.

[GAR 12] GARCIA-VILLORIA A., COROMINAS A., DELORME X., et al., "A branch and bound algorithm for the response time variability problem", *Journal of Scheduling*, pp. 1–10, 2012.

[GAV 82] GAVISH B., "Topological design of centralized computer networks formulation and algorithms", *Networks*, vol. 12, pp. 355–377, 1982.

[GAV 83] GAVISH B., "Formulation and algorithms for the capacitated minimal directed tree problem", *Journal of the Association Computing Machinery*, vol. 30, no. 1, pp. 118–132, 1983.

[GAV 91] GAVISH B., "Topological design telecommunications networks – local access design methods", *Annals of Operations Research*, vol. 33, pp. 17–71, 1991.

[GIL 66] GILMORE P.C., GOMORY R.E., "The theory and computation of knapsack functions", *Operations Research*, vol. 14, pp. 1045–1074, 1966.

[HAF 98] HANAFI S., FREVILLE A., "An efficient tabu search approach for the 0–1 multidimensional knapsack problem", *European Journal of Operational Research*, vol. 106, nos. 2–3, pp. 659–675, 16 April 1998.

[HAM 91] HAMACHER H.W., JNORNSTEN K., MALOLI F., Weighted k-cardinality trees, Technical Report no. 91.023, Department of Electronics, Polytechnic University of Milan, Italy, 1991.

[HAM 93] HAMACHER H.W., JNORNSTEN K., Optimal relinquishment according to the Norwegian petrol law: a combinatorial optimization approach, Technical Report no. 7/93, Norwegian School of Economics and Business Administration, Bergen, Norway, 1993.

[HAO 06a] HAOUARI M., CHAOUACHI J.S., "Upper and lower bounding strategies for the generalized minimum spanning tree problem", European Journal of Operational Research, vol. 171, pp. 632–647, 2006.

[HAO 06b] HAOUARI M., CHAOUACHI J.S., "A hybrid Lagrangian genetic algorithm for the prize collecting Steiner tree problem", *Computers & Operations Research*, vol. 33, pp. 1274–1288, 2006.

[KAP 66] KAPLAN S., "Solution of the Lorie-Savage and similar integer programming problems by the generalized Lagrange multiplier method", *Operations Research*, vol. 14, pp. 1130–1136, 1966.

[LO 08] LO S.T., CHEN R.M., HUANG Y.M., *et al.*, "Multiprocessor system scheduling with precedence and resource constraints using an enhanced ant colony system", *Expert Systems with Applications*, vol. 34, pp. 2071–2081, 2008.

[MAL 93] MALIK K., YU G., "A branch and bound algorithm for the capacitated minimum spanning tree problem", *Networks,* vol. 23, pp. 525–532, 1993.

[MYU] MYUNG Y.S., LEE C.H., TCHA D.W., "On the generalized minimum spanning tree problem", *Networks*, vol. 26, pp. 231–241.

[PAP 78] PAPADIMITRIOU C.H., "The complexity of the capacitated tree problem", *Networks*, vol. 8, pp. 217–230, 1978.

[PAP 82] PAPADIMITRIOU C.H., STEIGLITZ K., *Combinatorial Optimization: Algorithms and Complexity*, Prentice-Hall, Inc., Upper Saddle River, NJ, 1982.

[PHI 97] PHILPOTT A.B., WORMALD N.C., On the Optimal Extraction of Ore from an Open-Cast Mine, University of Auckland, New Zealand, 1997.

[REI 06] REIMANN M., LAUMANNS M., "Savings based ant colony optimization for the capacitated minimum spanning tree problem", *Computers & Operations Research*, vol. 33, pp. 1794–1822, 2006.

[TAK 80] TAKAHASHI H., MATSUYAMA A., "An approximate solution for the Steiner problem in graphs", *Mathematica Japonica,* vol. 24, pp. 573–577, 1980.

[TEM 07] TEMEL Ö., "The survey of the generalized assignment problem and its applications", *ABI/INFORM Global*, vol. 45, no. 3, pp. 123, August 2007.

[TAR 02] TARANTILIS C.D., KIRANOUDIS C.T., "Using a spatial decision support system for solving the vehicle routing problem", *Information & Management*, vol. 39, pp. 359–375, 2002.

[WAN 13] WANG Y., DE SCHUTTER B., VAN DEN BOOM T.J.J., *et al.*, Optimal trajectory planning for trains: a pseudospectral method and a mixed integer linear programming approach, Technical Report no. 13-004, Delft Center for Systems and Control, Delft University of Technology, 2013.

[ZHO 03] ZHOU G., GEN M., "A genetic algorithm approach on tree-like telecommunication network design problem", *Journal of the Operational Research Society*, vol. 54, no. 3, pp. 248–254, 2003.

Index

Other titles from

in

Computer Engineering

2014

BOULANGER Jean-Louis
Formal Methods Applied to Industrial Complex Systems

BOULANGER Jean-Louis
Formal Methods Applied to Complex Systems: Implementation of the B Method

GARDI Frédéric, BENOIST Thierry, DARLAY Julien, ESTELLON Bertrand, MEGEL Romain
Mathematical Programming Solver based on Local Search

OUSSALAH Mourad Chabane
Software Architecture 1

OUSSALAH Mourad Chabane
Software Architecture 2

QUESNEL Flavien
Scheduling of Large-scale Virtualized Infrastructures: Toward Cooperative Management

TOUATI Sid, DE DINECHIN Benoit
Advanced Backend Optimization

2013

ANDRÉ Etienne, SOULAT Romain
The Inverse Method: Parametric Verification of Real-time Embedded Systems

BOULANGER Jean-Louis
Safety Management for Software-based Equipment

DELAHAYE Daniel, PUECHMOREL Stéphane
Modeling and Optimization of Air Traffic

FRANCOPOULO Gil
LMF — Lexical Markup Framework

GHÉDIRA Khaled
Constraint Satisfaction Problems

ROCHANGE Christine, UHRIG Sascha, SAINRAT Pascal
Time-Predictable Architectures

WAHBI Mohamed
Algorithms and Ordering Heuristics for Distributed Constraint Satisfaction Problems

ZELM Martin *et al.*
Enterprise Interoperability

2012

ARBOLEDA Hugo, ROYER Jean-Claude
Model-Driven and Software Product Line Engineering

BLANCHET Gérard, DUPOUY Bertrand
Computer Architecture

BOULANGER Jean-Louis
Industrial Use of Formal Methods: Formal Verification

BOULANGER Jean-Louis
Formal Method: Industrial Use from Model to the Code

CALVARY Gaëlle, DELOT Thierry, SEDES Florence, TIGLI Jean-Yves
Computer Science and Ambient Intelligence

MAHOUT Vincent
Assembly Language Programming: ARM Cortex-M3 2.0: Organization, Innovation and Territory

MARLET Renaud
Program Specialization

SOTO Maria, SEVAUX Marc, ROSSI André, LAURENT Johann
Memory Allocation Problems in Embedded Systems: Optimization Methods

2011

BICHOT Charles-Edmond, SIARRY Patrick
Graph Partitioning

BOULANGER Jean-Louis
Static Analysis of Software: The Abstract Interpretation

CAFERRA Ricardo
Logic for Computer Science and Artificial Intelligence

HOMES Bernard
Fundamentals of Software Testing

KORDON Fabrice, HADDAD Serge, PAUTET Laurent, PETRUCCI Laure
Distributed Systems: Design and Algorithms

KORDON Fabrice, HADDAD Serge, PAUTET Laurent, PETRUCCI Laure
Models and Analysis in Distributed Systems

LORCA Xavier
Tree-based Graph Partitioning Constraint

TRUCHET Charlotte, ASSAYAG Gerard
Constraint Programming in Music

VICAT-BLANC PRIMET Pascale *et al.*
Computing Networks: From Cluster to Cloud Computing

LECOUTRE Christophe
Constraint Networks / Targeting Simplicity for Techniques and Algorithms

2008

BANÂTRE Michel, MARRÓN Pedro José, OLLERO Hannibal, WOLITZ Adam
Cooperating Embedded Systems and Wireless Sensor Networks

MERZ Stephan, NAVET Nicolas
Modeling and Verification of Real-time Systems

PASCHOS Vangelis Th
Combinatorial Optimization and Theoretical Computer Science: Interfaces and Perspectives

WALDNER Jean-Baptiste
Nanocomputers and Swarm Intelligence

2007

BENHAMOU Frédéric, JUSSIEN Narendra, O'SULLIVAN Barry
Trends in Constraint Programming

JUSSIEN Narendra
A to Z of Sudoku

2006

BABAU Jean-Philippe *et al.*
From MDD Concepts to Experiments and Illustrations – DRES 2006

HABRIAS Henri, FRAPPIER Marc
Software Specification Methods

MURAT Cecile, PASCHOS Vangelis Th
Probabilistic Combinatorial Optimization on Graphs

PANETTO Hervé, BOUDJLIDA Nacer
Interoperability for Enterprise Software and Applications 2006 / IFAC-IFIP I-ESA'2006

2005

GÉRARD Sébastien *et al.*
Model Driven Engineering for Distributed Real Time Embedded Systems

PANETTO Hervé
Interoperability of Enterprise Software and Applications 2005

Printed and bound by CPI Group (UK) Ltd, Croydon, CR0 4YY

10/09/2023

08111269-0001